Desert to Sea

10 Quilts from Australian Designers

Compiled by Jane Davidson

Desert to Sea
10 Quilts from Australian Designers
Copyright © 2013 Want it Need it Quilt

Published by Want it Need it Quilt
PO Box 77, Albany Creek QLD 4035, Australia
deserttoseaquilts@gmail.com

Acknowledgments
Art Director / Book Designer: Kaitlin Alexander, Jane Davidson
Editor: Jane Davidson
Pattern Designers: Betty Kerr, Cathy Underhill, Charlotte Dumesny, Danielle Aeuckens, Jane Davidson, Rachaeldaisy, Jeannette Bruce, Lorena Uriarte.

National Library of Australia Cataloguing – in – publication data

ISBN 978-0-9923-2180-2

Dedicated to Rhonda Kay Shallala

Quilts are a craft of love ... They provide warmth, comfort and memories ...

Contents

Desert to Sea

I find most Australian quilters are inherently eclectic in their style of quilting. They are not afraid to use bold colours and patterns in their designs. Maybe it is a reflection of the beauty that surrounds them and the diversity in our landscape and culture that inspires them to create such beautiful and unique quilts.

Longing to share our Australian talent with the world, I embarked on a plan to self publish a book introducing seven Aussie quilters and myself. I met all these passionate quilters on-line through their blogs. Each has their own story to tell, injecting elements of their personalities, unique styles and favourite techniques into their designs.

General Information

The book is aimed at the intermediate to advanced quilter. It is assumed that you will be familiar with the techniques used in each pattern. The individual designers will be hosting tips and tricks on their blogs to assist you. Contact information for each designer can be found in the book in section - *'Designers'.*

Some information to get you started:

- ❀ It is important to read all instructions before commencing a project.

- ❀ All seams are ¼" unless otherwise specified.

- ❀ Cutting instructions are based on 40" width of fabric, unless otherwise specified.

- ❀ The basic requirements for each project include general sewing tools for all projects include a sewing machine with ¼" foot, scissors, thread, quilters ruler, cutting mat, rotary cutter, pins, seam ripper.

- ❀ All measurements for requirements are listed in imperial and metric. The cutting instructions and block sizes are in imperial measurements only. A table has been provided for conversion of imperial to metric.

- ❀ When printing templates, do not have printer set to 'scale' or 'fit to page'. Enlarge as indicated for each template.

Conversion chart

To Convert	To	Multiply By
Inches	Centimetres	2.54
Centimetres	Inches	0.4
Yards	Metres	0.9
Metres	Yards	1.1

Key terms used in the book

Abbreviation	Description	Abbreviation	Description
WOF	Width of fabric	yd	Yard
HST	Half square triangle	"	Inches
QST	Quarter square triangle	'	Feet
FQ	Fat quarter	cm	Centimetre
F8	Fat eighth	m	Metre

Lorena Uriarte

Finished Size: 83" x 84" (2.11 m x 2.14 m)

Requirements

- Tumbling blocks: 2 ½ yards (2.2m) each of assorted light, medium and dark fabrics.

- Setting and corner triangles: 1/3 yard (30 cm) of medium fabrics and 5/8 yard (55cm) of dark fabrics.

- Small Circle: 57 – 3" x 3" squares of assorted fabrics.

- Medium Circle: 66 – 4" x 4" squares of assorted fabrics.

- Large Circle: 81 – 5" x 5" squares of assorted fabrics.

- Binding - ¾ yard (60 cm)

- Backing - 5 yards (4.5 m)

- Batting: 90" x 90" (2.3 m x 2.3 m)

- Appliqué Glue

- Freezer Paper

- Pencil / Chalk Pen

Preparation

The pieces for this project are cut from templates.

Note: Acrylic Templates for this project can be ordered via Lorena's blog site.

Tumbling Blocks and Setting Triangles

- From template plastic or sturdy cardboard, cut one of each of the templates A, B, C and D. Label them clearly with the letter and the grain line direction on the right side up.

Circles

- From template plastic or sturdy cardboard, cut one of each of the templates E, F and G. Label them clearly with the letter on the right side up.

Cutting

Tumbling Blocks

Using template A, cut from the assorted light, dark and medium assorted fabrics (Piece A):

- 72 light diamonds.

- 68 medium diamonds.

- 72 dark diamonds.

Cut from the binding fabric:

- 9 – 2 ¼" x WOF strips.

Cutting the diamond shapes

1. Place the Diamond Template A with the grain line indicator running parallel to the selvedge.

2. Trim away the selvedge and discard.

3. Place your Diamond template A along the cut edge and place another long ruler along the outside edge. Use Template A to cut the correct width.

4. Cut the diamonds along the width of the fabric.

> Hint: You may cut several layers at once to speed up the process.

Mark the Diamonds

The diamonds are sewn together using Y-seams. To help with accurately sewing Y-seams, you may wish to mark the seam intersection points on the wrong side of the fabric. These will indicate the start and finish of each seam.

Setting Triangles

1. Using template B, cut 8 medium tone triangles making sure that the grain line marked on the template is parallel with the fabric selvedge (Piece B).

2. Using template C, cut 14 dark tone half-diamonds, making sure the grain runs as indicated on the template. This is important in creating a flat edge for the quilt. (Piece C).

3. Using template D, cut 4 dark-tone triangles in two pairs, two with the template facing up and two with the template facing down. This creates two pairs of mirrored triangles, used to form the corners of the quilt (Piece D).

Appliqué

This quilt was made using the freezer-paper technique to appliqué the circle pieces to the diamonds. This technique allows accurate placement of the circle edge, giving an accurate circle outline when the three pieces come together.

Prepare the appliquéd circle pieces

There are 27 large circles, 22 medium and 19 small circles. Each circle requires three equal pieces. To enhance the quilt's 3-D effect, choose one each of a light, medium and dark fabric to make each circle, and appliqué them to the corresponding light, medium and dark segments of the tumbling blocks.

> Hint: Freezer paper can be used multiple times. Appliqué small groups of circle segments, remove the freezer paper and use again. Use a lower setting on your iron to press the freezer paper onto the fabric. This will preserve the shape of the freezer paper template.

Large Circle

1. Trace template G onto dull side of freezer paper. Cut on pencil line.

2. Press the shiny side of the freezer paper template G on wrong size of the 5" x 5" squares of assorted fabrics. Cut out adding a ¼" seam allowance all around.

3. Press ¼" seam over the curved edge only. The straight sides will be included in the seam.

Medium Circle

1. Trace Template F onto dull side of freezer paper. Cut on pencil line.

2. Press the shiny side of the freezer paper template F, on wrong size of the 4" x 4" squares of assorted fabrics. Cut out adding a ¼" seam allowance all around.

3. Press ¼" seam over the curved edge only. The straight sides will be included in the seam.

Small Circle

1. Trace template E onto dull side of freezer paper. Cut on pencil line.

2. Press the shiny side of the freezer paper template E on wrong size of the 3" x 3" squares of assorted fabrics. Cut out adding a ¼" seam allowance all around.

3. Press ¼" seam over the curved edge only. The straight sides will be included in the seam.

Appliqué Circles

1. Line up the straight edges of the circle piece with the edges of the diamond. Using a few dabs of appliqué glue, secure the circle piece onto the diamond piece.

2. Using small stitches with matching thread, appliqué same sized circle pieces onto diamonds.

3. After all circle pieces are appliquéd onto background diamonds, trim away the excess fabric underneath leaving a ¼" seam allowance and remove the freezer paper. This reduces the bulk in the Y-seam when the diamonds are pieced together.

Block Assembly

Tumbling Blocks

1. Carefully select the order that you arrange the light, medium and dark diamonds of your tumbling block. To achieve the 3-D effect in this quilt, it must appear the light source is coming from one direction. Use the quilt outline at the back of the book to plan your fabrics and layout.

2. Select 2 diamonds, 1 medium and 1 dark tone.

3. Match the points where the two circle pieces meet on the edge of the medium and dark diamonds.

4. Pin or glue that point in the seam allowance.

5. Sew the two pieces together using the markings, which show the seam's start and finish points. Make locking stitches at the start and finish of each seam.

6. Take a light value diamond. Match the circle piece to the circle piece edge on the medium diamond.

7. Glue or pin to match the seams. Sew the medium and light pieces together using the markings, which show the seam's start and finish points. Make locking stitches at the start and finish of each seam.

8. Complete the tumbling block by sewing the light piece to the dark piece. Check circle edges and press the diamond seams clockwise. The fabric at the centre of the Y-seam should fan open in a swirl, reducing bulk at that point.

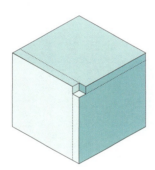

9. Make 68 blocks.

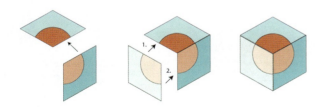

Half Hexagon Blocks

These are the setting blocks made from templates A and B.

1. Sew Piece B to a dark tone Piece A. Start and finish at the ¼" marking on the pieces. Make 4.

2. Sew Piece B to a light tone Piece A. Start and finish at the ¼" marking on the pieces. Make 4.

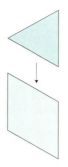

Quilt Assembly

1. Arrange all blocks on a design wall, arranging all the different sized circle blocks as in the quilt layout diagram. Tumbling block rows 1, 3, 5, 7 and 9 will have 8 blocks. Rows 2, 4, 6, and 8 will have 7 blocks.

2. Sew 8 blocks into a row for the first row.

3. Sew 7 blocks for the second row, pivoting at the ¼" marking on each intersection.

4. Continue until you have five rows of 8 and four rows of 7 blocks, making sure all the diamonds of equal tone are facing in the same direction. Sew the half hexagon blocks to the sides of rows 2, 4, 6 and 8, making sure to follow the quilt layout diagram so that the half-hexagons of medium and dark tones are along the left hand side and the medium and light tones are on the right. Sew the 14 setting half-diamonds (Piece C) to the top and bottom rows of the quilt. Carefully pin and sew one seam at a time. Make locking stitches at the start and finish of each seam.

5. Sew the quarter-diamond (Piece D) to each corner.

6. Sew the rows into pairs with one row remaining.

7. Sew two sets of pairs together and add the last row.

8. Press the Y-seams between blocks to one side, fanning the centre seam to reduce bulk.

Finishing the Quilt

1. Cut the backing fabric into 2 – 2 ½ yard pieces, remove selvages and sew together to yield 1 – 86" x 90" backing piece.

2. Layer the backing, batting and quilt top.

3. Baste and quilt as desired.

4. Sew together the 9 binding strips and bind the quilt.

Opal Essence was custom quilted by Michele Turner.

Jane Davidson

Finished Block Size 24" x 24" (58.8 cms x 58.8 cms)

Finished Quilt Size 72" x 72" (1.83 m x 1.83 m)

Requirements

Width of fabric (WOF) calculated at 40"

- ✿ 1 yard (90cm) each of 7 neutral fabrics
- ✿ 1 ½" yards (1.35m) red fabric
- ✿ 1 yd (90cm) orange fabric
- ✿ ½ yd (50cm) grey fabric
- ✿ ¼ yd (25cm) lime Fabric
- ✿ Binding fabric - ¾ yd (75cm)
- ✿ Backing fabric - 4 ¾ yards (4.3 m)
- ✿ Batting - 78"x 78" (1.9 x 1.9 m)
- ✿ Template plastic
- ✿ Silver gel pen
- ✿ Appliqué glue
- ✿ Optional – EZ Quilting TriTool™

Preparation

Prepare the Appliqué Pieces

1. Lightly trace template D onto right side of the orange fabric with a silver gel pen.

2. Cut around shape leaving a ¼" seam allowance.

3. Make 36

4. Repeat for template E (grey fabric) and template F (lime fabric).

Cutting

From each of the 1 yard of neutral fabrics cut:

- ✂ 5 – 3 ½" x WOF strips.
- ✂ Using template C, cut 576 triangles (Piece C).
- ✂ 36 – template B (Piece B).

From the red fabric cut:

- ✂ 36 - template A (Piece A)

From the binding fabric cut:

- ✂ 8 – 2 ½" x WOF strips.

Quilting by Jane Davidson

Block Assembly

Pyramid Block

1. Lay out 16 triangles (Piece C).

2. Join 6 pairs of triangles (Piece C) together. Press seams open.

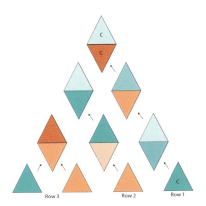

3. Sew corner triangles and pairs into 3 rows.

4. Join three rows together. Press seams to one side in opposite direction for each row.

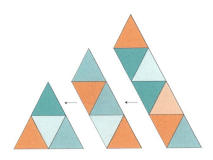

5. Make 36 pyramids.

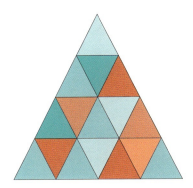

Appliqué Block

1. Sew Piece A to Piece B. Open seam.

2. Make 36.

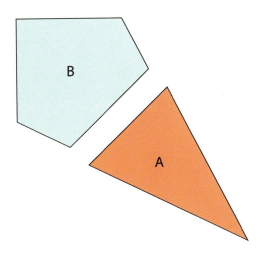

Assembling the Block

1. Join a pyramid block to an appliqué block. Make 4 pairs.

2. Join 2 pairs together to make half a block. Press seams in one direction.

3. Join 2 halves. Press seam open.

4. Make 9 blocks.

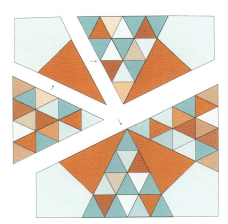

Appliqué

1. Using the prepared appliqué pieces D, E and F, finger press the ¼" seam under.

2. Place a dab of appliqué glue on the wrong side of each piece and position on block. The points of each finished melon shape should touch the edge of the appliqué block and line-up with the seams of each pyramid row.

3. Using the silver pen line as a guide, stitch each piece to the background block with matching thread.

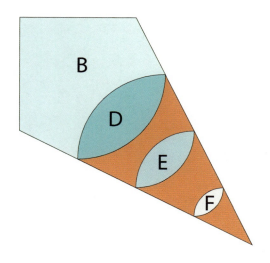

Quilt Assembly

1. Lay out the 9 blocks.

2. Join 3 blocks together to make 1 row. Press seams open.

3. Make 3 rows and join. Press seams open.

Finishing the Quilt

1. Cut the backing fabric into 2 pieces and sew together. Press seam open.

2. Layer, baste and quilt as desired.

3. Bind the quilt.

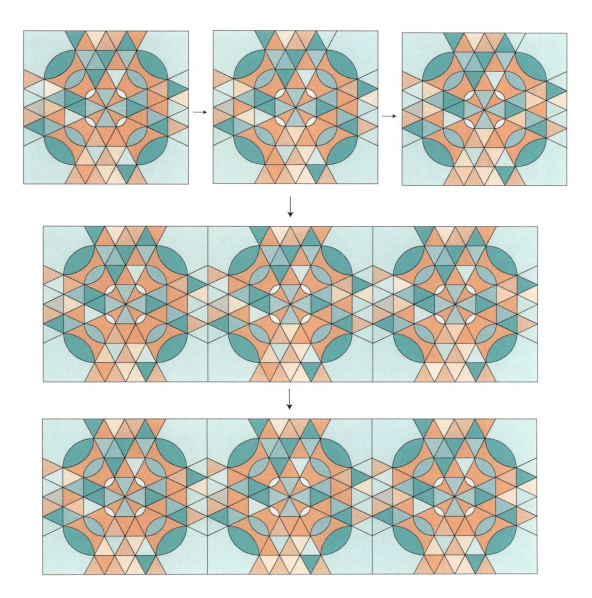

Around the Rainbow

Danielle Aeuckens

Finished Size: 63" x 73" (1.6 m x 1.85 m)

Requirements

- ❀ 2 – 6" x 6" (15cm x 15cm) squares of different fabric for centre circles.

- ❀ 8 – fat eighths of assorted low volume or text print fabrics with white backgrounds.

- ❀ 45 – fat eighths of assorted prints in 6 different colourways (blue, green, orange, yellow, pink and purple)

- ❀ 1 – fat quarter solid in white or cream (this fabric sits behind the appliquéd wheel and will not be seen in the final quilt).

- ❀ Binding fabric: 3/4 yd (75cm)

- ❀ Backing fabric: 4 yds (4 m)

- ❀ Batting: 70" x 80" (1.9 m x 2.2 m)

- ❀ Matching thread

- ❀ Needles for hand appliqué

- ❀ Plain A4 paper for drafting a wedge template

- ❀ Fabric glue stick

- ❀ 12" - 18 ° Dresden wedge ruler

- ❀ Cardboard for cutting circle templates (cereal box cardboard is fine)

- ❀ Aluminium foil

Cutting

Background

Cut from 45 – fat eighths of assorted prints:

- ✂ 100 – 4" x 9 ½" rectangles (Piece A).

- ✂ 23 – 4" x 5" rectangles (Piece B).

Cut from the 8 – fat eighths of low volume text prints:

- ✂ 23 – 4" x 9 ½" rectangles (Piece A).

- ✂ 3 – 4" x 5" rectangles (Piece B).

Cut from the fat quarter cream/white solid:

- ✂ 7 – 4" x 9 ½" rectangles (Piece A).

Cut from the binding fabric:

- ✂ 8 – 2 ¼" x WOF strips.

Colour Wheel

Cut from 45 – fat eighths of assorted prints:

- ✂ 20 – 3" x 2" rectangles (Piece C).

- ✂ 20 – 2" x 3" (Piece D).

- ✂ 20 – 2" x 4" (Piece E).

- ✂ 20 – 2" x 5" (Piece F).

- ✂ 20 – 3" x 6" (Piece G)

Tools

To piece the colour wheel in the centre use a 12"- 18 degree Dresden ruler. This creates a wheel consisting of 20 wedges. If you have a smaller ruler, make your own template by tracing onto a sheet of paper and extending the lines. To determine the height of your Dresden, draw a 12" line from the base of your Dresden template.

Quilt Assembly

Background

1. Using a design wall, lay out Piece A and Piece B. Move pieces around until the desired colourwash effect is achieved.

2. Sew the quilt together row by row. Pair rows together, and then sections until you have two halves. Finally piece the two halves together.

> Hint: A design wall is very useful in making this quilt; if you don't have one, create a large space on the floor to lay out the pieces and move them around. Lay a piece of batting on the floor before you put down the pieces. If you need to pack up in the middle of making the quilt, you can carefully roll up the batting and keep the pieces together. Take pictures of your lay out as you go so as to remember where the pieces are placed in case they decide to move themselves around.

Making the colour wheel

Colouring outlines for the background and wheel are found in the section 'Quilt outlines to colour'.

1. The centre colour wheel is planned in a similar manner to the background, with the colours gradually changing around the wheel. A degree of trial and error is used to put the pieces together to achieve the right result. Work on three wedges at a time, taking care to spread the colours and not have cuts of the same print appearing next to each other.

2. Finger press Pieces C, D, E, F and G in half lengthways.

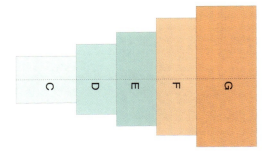

3. Sew pieces C, D, E, F and G together. Press seams to one side. Alternate the pressing direction for each wedge so that the seams will nest when the colour wheel is assembled.

4. Lay the 18 ° Dresden wedge ruler on the pieced wedge. The base of the 18 ° Dresden wedge ruler should be centred on the bottom edge of the pieced wedge. Trim excess. The height of each wedge is 10".

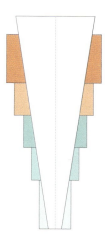

5. Make 20.

6. Lay out the wedges, taking care with colour placement as you approach the last few wedges to ensure that the colours blend back towards those of the first wedges.

7. Sew together in pairs.

8. Sew 5 pair together to make half a wheel. Make 2.

9. Sew 2 halves together. Press all seams to the side. The seams at the centre of the wheel will get bulky. These will be covered by the appliqué circles.

Appliquéing the colour wheel to the background

1. Find the centre of the background and mark it lightly with a pencil.

2. On the wrong side of the colour wheel, fold over the outer edge by ¼" and press. If you wish you could also dab a little glue to secure the seam allowance even more.

3. Dab glue on the back of the wheel and lay it onto the centre of the quilt. Secure well with pins to stop the wheel from shifting as you appliqué.

4. Using a blind stitch, sew the wheel in place at the outer edge.

5. Turn the quilt over and carefully trim the excess fabric away from the back behind the colour wheel, leaving an allowance of at least ¼". This reduces bulk to make quilting easier.

Prepare the centre circles.

The centre circles will be appliquéd after quilting.

1. Cut from cardboard 3.5" (template A) and 5" (template B) circles.

2. Use template A and B to trace circles on the wrong side of the 2 - 6" x 6" pieces of fabric. Add a ¼" seam allowance and cut out the circles.

3. Lay a square of aluminium foil, shiny side down, on the ironing board.

4. Place the fabric circle right side down in the centre of the foil, and place the cardboard circle on top.

5. Fold the foil edge over tightly all the way around the circle, pressing well with your fingers, then with the iron.

6. Carefully remove the foil and cardboard and your fabric circle is ready to sew with a neatly pressed turned edge.

Finishing the Quilt

1. Layer, baste and quilt as desired. Danielle quilted in the ditch around the edge of the colour wheel as well as in the seam between each of the wedges and quilted a dense swirl pattern over the white background surrounding the wheel. As a finishing touch, Danielle hand-quilted in various colours of Perle 8 thread ¼" away from the seam along the coloured bricks.

2. Appliqué the prepared 3 ½" and 5" circles to the centre of the wheel. Hand quilt around the inner circle.

3. Bind the quilt.

Photography and quilting by Danielle Aeuckens

Geishas In the Night

Betty Kerr

Finished quilt size: 72" x 84" (1.88 m x 2.20 m)

Requirements

- ❀ Background Fabric: 3 ½" yards (3.2 m) of Japanese Indigo Blue

- ❀ Kimono Background: 1 ½ yards (1 ¼ m) light fabric

- ❀ Kimono body: 4 - Fat Quarters of bright Japanese prints

- ❀ Kimono appliqué: assorted scraps of Japanese prints

- ❀ Large octagons: 4 – 15" x 15" squares Japanese prints

- ❀ Centre squares and octagon border: 2 – fat quarters of assorted Japanese prints

- ❀ Centre octagon: 1 - fat quarter of solid fabric

- ❀ Border 1: ¾ yard (75 cm) of indigo Japanese border print

- ❀ Border 2: 2 ¼ yards (2.1 m)

- ❀ Binding: 1 yard (90 cm)

- ❀ Small hexagons: 18 - 2 ½" x 2 ½" (6.4 cm x 6.4 cm) squares of assorted Japanese fabrics

- ❀ Backing fabric: 80" x 92" (1.8 m x 2.4 m)

- ❀ Batting: 78" x 90" (2.0 m x 2.3 m)

- ❀ Matching machine threads for general sewing and appliqué.

- ❀ White Japanese sashiko cotton thread or white embroidery floss.

- ❀ Japanese sashiko needle, or any large needle with a large eye.

- ❀ 1 ½ yard (1.5 m) Light weight Fusible Web

- ❀ Water erasable marker

- ❀ Quilter's transfer paper

- ❀ Template Plastic

- ❀ Photocopy paper

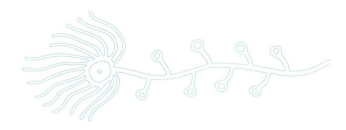

Cutting

From the blue background fabric cut:

- ✂ 2 – 60 ½ " x Width of Fabric (WOF).

From Border Fabric 1 cut:

- ✂ 4 – 4 1 /2" x Width of fabric (WOF).

From border Fabric 2 cut:

- ✂ 4 – 6 ½" x Length of fabric.

From the kimono background fabric cut:

- ✂ 4 – 20" x 20" squares.

From binding fabric cut:

- ✂ 9 – 2 ½" x Width of Fabric (WOF).

Appliqué

Appliqué Preparation

1. Lay out all the fabrics selected for the kimonos. Be sure the fabrics are not similar so that each piece of the kimono stands out. Frequently, Japanese textiles include gold print. These prints are perfect for the kimonos. The kimonos should feature prominently on the quilt.

2. Place the selected kimono fabrics in 4 groups.

   Note: The octagons need to be different in colour toning from the kimonos. Accurately cutting the octagons is crucial to the correct assembly of the centre of the block of the quilt.

Appliqué Kimonos

1. Photocopy the kimono pattern pieces Templates A – F.

2. Trace all Template pieces onto the dull side of the fusible web.

3. Cut 1/8" from the edge pencil line.

4. Using manufacturers instructions, fuse onto wrong side of kimono fabric.

5. Cut out the pieces on the pencil line.

6. Remove backing paper.

7. Place the pieces together to see that they all fit correctly and you are happy with your choice of colours.

8. Take a 20" x 20" square of kimono background fabric and fold in half, then in quarters and press with fingers to find the centre.

9. Position the kimono appliqué pieces onto the background fabric in the following order:

   1. Collar (Piece E)

   2. Left and right outside panel (Piece C)

   3. Left and right inside panel (Piece B)

   4. Body (Piece A)

   5. Left and right sleeve (Piece D)

   6. Waist (Piece F)

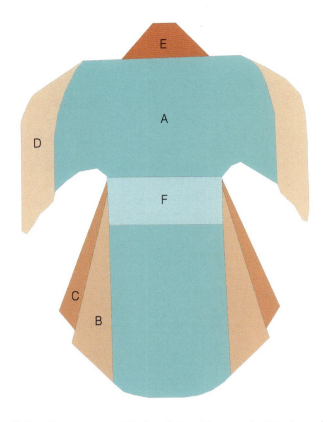

Note: The kimono appliqué must be centrally placed in the 20" x 20" backing square. To achieve this use the fold lines to centre the kimono. Fold template A lengthways in half and match with folded line of background square. Position the kimono so it is an equal distance from the top and bottom and from both sides.

10. When you are happy with the layout of the kimono, carefully remove Pieces A, D and F.

11. Fuse Pieces E, B and C to the background squares. Using a matching thread, appliqué the edges that are exposed (edges that will not be placed under other layers).

12. Fuse and appliqué Pieces A, D and F to complete the kimono.

13. Make 4.

14. Using a 9" length of string and a pencil, make an 18" circle on joined photocopy paper. Finger press the paper circle in half, then in quarters to find the centre.

15. Pin the paper circle onto the wrong side of kimono background square, using the folds to match the centre of the background square.

16. Cut ¼" from the edge of the paper circle. Repeat for remaining 3 kimono blocks.

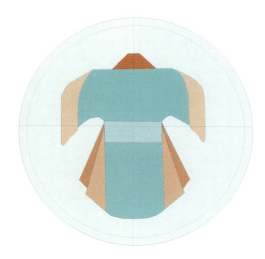

> Hint: Shorten the width of the appliqué stitch as you approach a tight curve or point.

Centre Octagon

The centre octagon is prepared and placed aside until the background and borders are assembled.

1. Make template H and I.

2. Trace template H onto wrong side of the solid fabric and cut out on pencil line. (Piece H).

3. Trace template I onto wrong side of fabric and cut on pencil line. Cut 8 pieces (Piece I).

4. With right sides together, pin the long edge of Piece I on one edge of the centre octagon.

5. Stitch the seam partway as shown. Press seams away from the centre.

6. Pin the next Piece I onto the centre octagon. Sew the complete seam.

7. Continue clockwise around the octagon to join the 8 strips total.

8. End by completing the partial seam and press.

9. Using a ruler, trim away excess fabric.

Sashiko

1. Selecting your favourite sashiko design, photocopy the pattern. The design must fit into a 7 ½" circle.

2. Using a flat surface, place down the octagon right side up.

3. Place the transfer paper with right side down. Place the sashiko pattern on top.

4. Using a pen slowly trace the sashiko pattern onto the fabric, making sure the lines are coming through without tearing the paper. Be sure to centre the design.

5. Thread your needle with the white sashiko thread. Start with a knot on the end, commence stitching, trying to make each stitch and space as even as possible, the length of stitch being 1/8" preferably. Do a practice run on a piece first to get the feel and look. To finish off, thread through the last 5 stitches on the back.

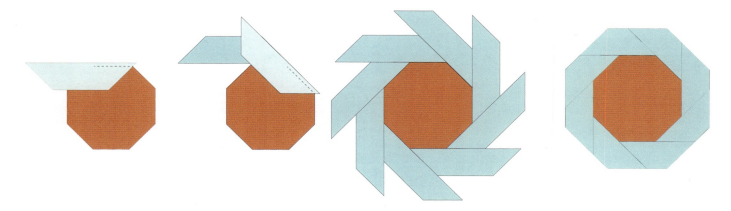

Assembling the quilt

Background and Borders

1. Sew together the 2 backing pieces lengthways. Press seam open.

2. Starting at the centre seam, measure 32 ¼" from the seam above and below. Trim back to 60 ½" x 64 ½".

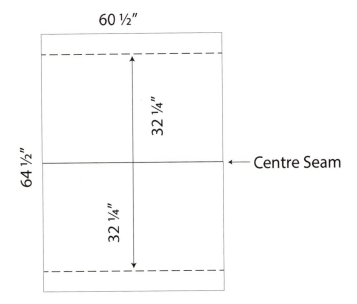

3. Take 2 strips of Border 1 fabric. Remove selvages and join the pieces. Match pattern as close as possible to hide seam. Trim to 4 ½" x 60 ½".

4. Make 2.

5. Sew to top and bottom of background piece.

6. Take 2 border 2 strips and trim back to 6 ½" x 60 ½" strips.

7. Sew to top and bottom of border 1.

8. Trim 2 border 2 strips to 6 ½" x 84 ½".

9. Sew to left and right side of quilt.

Appliqué
Octagons and Squares

> Note: Accuracy is important when cutting and preparing the ¼" seam on the octagons and squares.

1. Trace template G onto the wrong side of the 4 – 15" x 15" squares and cut out on pencil line. Cut out 4 Piece G.

2. Trace template J onto wrong side of assorted fat quarters of Japanese fabrics and cut out on pencil line. Cut out 4 Piece J.

3. Mark accurately, a ¼" seam on the right side of the fabric to use as a guide when pressing the seam allowance over on the shapes.

4. Press a ¼" seam.

Assemble centre appliqué

1. Using the centre seam of the blue background fabric, assemble the octagons and squares starting with the centre octagon.

2. Pin and baste all pieces onto the background, remembering to accurately position all pieces so that the finished appliqué block is centred on the quilt top.

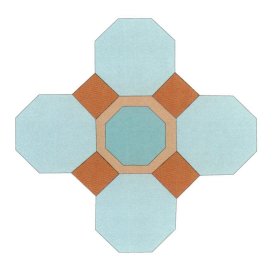

3. Using your favourite method of appliqué, sew to centre of quilt top.

4. Referring to photo of quilt for placement, lay quilt top on design wall or floor to pin and baste your 4 kimonos into their correct positions, overlapping onto outer border and panels.

5. Using the erasable marker, draw an accurate ¼" seam allowance on the right side of the kimono circle. Turn under seam allowance and appliqué to background.

Sashiko Designs

Sashiko designs are found in the *'Template'* section of the book.

1. Transfer the crane design onto the background fabric above and below the centre appliqué block.

2. Stitch the crane designs onto the background fabric.

3. Create your own water design. Transfer the water line designs onto the background fabric, positioning the design between the top and bottom kimono appliqués on both the left and right hand side of the quilt top.

Small Hexagons

1. Using template K, cut out 18 hexagons from the assorted 2 ½" x 2 ½" squares.

2. Press ¼" seam allowance to back of hexagon. Pin and baste hexagons along the stitched water lines. See quilt layout for guidance.

Finishing the Quilt

1. Layer the quilt top, batting and backing and baste. Stitch in the ditch lines along borders and panels and quilt as desired.

2. Bind quilt, label and enjoy.

Ladies Day at the Races

Jane Davidson

Finished Block Size: 8" x 8" (20.3 cm x 20.3 cm)

Finished Quilt Size: 64 ½" x 64 ½" (1.64 m x 1.64 m)

Requirements

- 13 – fat quarters of assorted solids
- ½ yard (50 cm) black polka dot fabric
- ¾ yard (75 cm) black on white text fabric
- ½ yard (50 cm) white on black text fabric
- 33 – fat eighths of assorted polka dot fabric
- 28 – 10" x 10" squares of assorted large print fabric
- ¾ yard (75 cm) binding fabric
- Backing: 4 ¼ yards (3.8 m)
- Batting: 72" x 72" (1.83 m x 1.83 m)

Cutting

Diamond Block

From the black polka dot fabric cut:

- 2 – 2 ⅜" x width of fabric strips. Cut into 30 – 2 ⅜" x 2 ⅜" squares (Piece A).

- 1 – 3 ⅞" x width of fabric strip. Cut into 8 – 3 ⅞" x 3 ⅞" squares. Cut squares on the diagonal twice to yield 30 triangles (Piece B).

From the black on white text fabric cut:

- 2 – 2 ⅜" x width of fabric strips. Cut into 30 – 2 ⅜" x 2 ⅜" squares (Piece A).

- 1 – 3 ⅞" x width of fabric strip. Cut into 8 – 3 ⅞" x 3 ⅞" squares. Cut squares on diagonal twice to yield 30 triangles (Piece B).

Stripe Block

From each assorted fat quarters of solids cut:

- 4 – 2 ½" x 8 ½" rectangle (Piece C).

Cross Block

From 5 fat quarters of assorted solid fabrics cut:

- 2 each - 1 ½" x 13" rectangles (Piece D).

From 5 fat eighths of assorted polka dot fabric cut:

- 5 – 8 ½" x 8 ½" squares (Piece E).

Checker Block

From the white on black text fabric cut:

- 4 – 2 ½" x width of fabric (Piece F).

From the black on white text fabric cut:

- 4 – 2 ½" x width of fabric (Piece F).

4 – Patch block

From each of the 10 Fat Quarters of assorted solid fabric cut:

- 2 – 4 ½" x 4 ½" squares (Piece G).

Jockey Silks Block

> Note: The jockey silks blocks are paper pieced (foundation pieced). The cutting instructions for each segment are based on the sizes used to piece the block.

From each of 28 – 10" x 10" squares of assorted large print fabric cut:

- 1 – 6" x 6" squares (B4).

- 1– 2" x 6" rectangles (C2).

From each of 28 Fat Eighths of assorted polka dot fabric cut:

- 2 – 2" x 3" rectangles (A1 and B3).

- 2 – 2 ½" x 6" rectangles (B1 and A3).

- 2 – 2" x 4 ½" rectangles (C1 and C3).

- 2 – 2" x 9" rectangles (E1 and F1).

- 2 – 1 ½" x 4 ½" rectangles (D1 and D3).

From each assorted solid fabrics cut:

- 2 – 2" x 6" rectangles (B2 and A2).

- 1 – 1 ½" x 3 ½" rectangle (D2).

From the binding fabric cut:

✂ 8 – 2 ½" x width of fabric strips.

Block Assembly

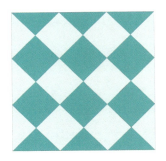

Diamond Block

1. Lay out the squares (Piece A) and triangles (Piece B).

2. Sew each row and then sew rows together. Press seams open.

3. Make 5

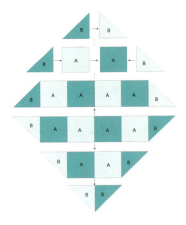

Stripe Block

1. Select 2 pair of contrasting solids of Piece C.

2. Using Diagram 3 as a guide, lay out the rectangles (Piece C).

3. Sew the 4 – Piece C together lengthways. Press seams open.

4. Make 13.

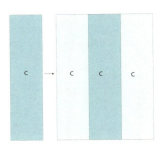

Cross Block

1. Select 1 of Piece E and a pair of contrasting Piece D.

2. Taking Piece E, cut once on the diagonal. Finger press both triangles in half to mark the centre.

3. Finger press Piece D in half to mark the centre.

4. Sew Piece D to one triangle. Use the pressed marks to line up the pieces. Sew the other triangle to Piece D, once again using the pressed marks to line up all 3 pieces.

5. Cut a diagonal line from the opposite corners. Press both triangles in half to mark the centre.

6. Finger press the other Piece D in half to mark the centre.

7. Sew the second Piece D to the centre of both triangles. Use the pressed marks to line up all 3 pieces.

8. Make 5.

Checker Block

1. Sew 4 – 2 ½" x width of fabric together lengthwise, alternating black and white text prints (Piece F). Press seams open. Make 2.

2. Cut 16 – 2 ½" strips from each strip set.

3. Make 32 strips.

4. Sew 4 rows together for each block. Flip each second strip to create the checker pattern. Press seams open.

5. Make 8.

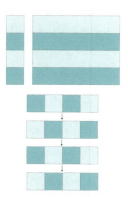

4 –Patch Block

1. Select 2 pair of contrasting Piece G.

2. Using Diagram 8 as a guide, layout 4 – Piece G.

3. Sew pairs together to make one row. Press seams open.

4. Sew rows together. Press seams open.

5. Make 5.

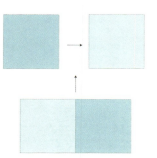

Jockey Silks Block

Note: Don't trim back the outer edges until the block is completed.

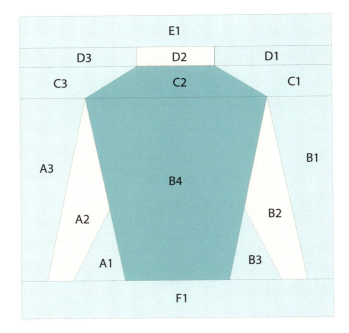

1. Make 28 copies of the paper piecing pattern. Cut out each segment and place into 28 piles.

2. Paper piece each section.

3. Join sections.

4. On completion of block, trim back to 8 ½" x 8 ½" square, making sure you are consistent in the positioning and trimming of each block.

5. Remove paper.

6. Make 28.

Hint: If you are not familiar with paper piecing, there are many great tutorials, books and videos available for this technique. Paper piecing, also known as foundation piecing, can be performed using paper or freezer paper.

Photography by Brian Cassey
Quilting by Jane Davidson

Quilt Assembly

1. Using a design wall, lay out 8 rows of 8 blocks each.

2. Sew 8 blocks together to make a row. Press seams open.

3. Sew rows together. Press seams open.

Finishing the Quilt

1. Cut backing yardage into 2 – 76 ½" pieces.

2. Sew 2 pieces together lengthwise using a ½" seam allowance. Press seam open.

3. Layer, baste and quilt as desired.

4. Bind, label and enjoy your quilt.

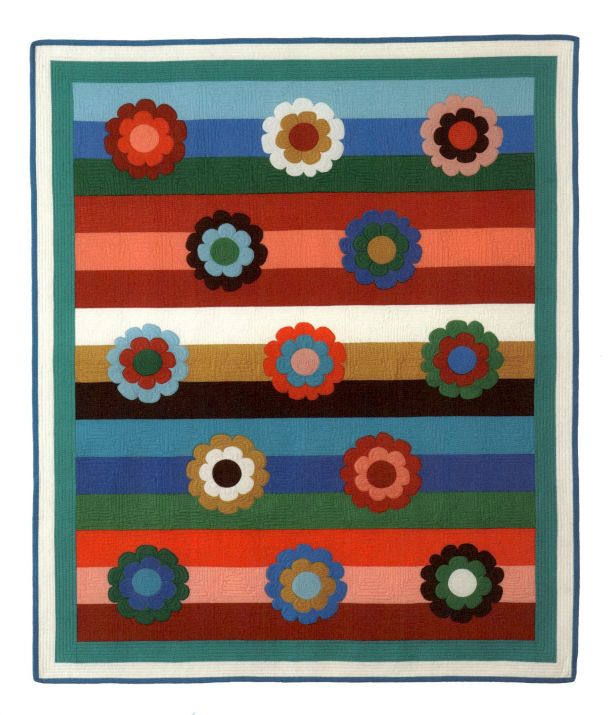

Vintage Flowers

Cathy Underhill

Finished Quilt Size 49" x 59 ½" (1.23 m x 1.50 m)

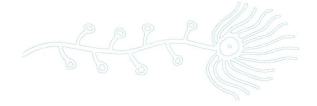

Requirements

- 🌸 ½ yd (50 cm), each of 15 solid fabrics (deep red, medium pink, salmon orange, green, blue, dark aqua, dark brown, gold, cream, dark pink, musk pink, dark salmon, dark green, medium blue, aqua)

- 🌸 Border 1: ½ yd (50 cm) teal green border fabric

- 🌸 Border 2: ½ yd (50 cm) extra cream border fabric ¾ yd (70 cm) blue fabric binding fabric

- 🌸 Fusible webbing: 1 ¾ yd (1.6 metres)

- 🌸 Backing fabric: 2 ¾ yds (2.7 metres)

- 🌸 Batting: 68" x 80" (1.7 x 2 metres)

- 🌸 Coloured machine threads to match fabric colours (alternatively, use medium grey, medium tan and cream thread)

- 🌸 Fabric glue stick (washable)

- 🌸 Pencil

- 🌸 Rotary cutter, ruler, mat

- 🌸 Scissors

- 🌸 Masking tape or clips

- 🌸 Basting safety pins (optional)

- 🌸 Sewing machine with darning foot (optional)

Cutting

Background

Cut from each of the 15 solid fabrics:

- ✂ 1 - 4" x 42 " strips.

Flowers

Cut from a selection of the 15 solids:

- ✂ 13 – 8 ½" x 8 ½" squares (Template A)

- ✂ 13 – 6 ½" x 6 ½" squares (Template B)

- ✂ 13 – 4 ½" x 4 ½" squares (Template C)

Border 1

Cut from the teal green fabric:

- ✂ 5 – 2 ½" x WOF strips.

Border 2

Cut from the extra cream fabric:

- ✂ 6 - 2" x WOF strips.

Backing

- ✂ Cut 2 – 13" x WOF strips.

- ✂ Cut 1 – 66" x WOF rectangle.

Binding

- ✂ Cut 6 - 2 ¾" x WOF strips.

Quilt Assembly

Background

1. Referring to colour photo, lay out strips, noting colour design. Colour design is worked in groups of 3 strips.

   For example: 3 strips of reds, pinks, salmons.

2. Working from top of quilt carefully pin strips together lengthways and sew together. Press seams toward bottom of quilt.

The Flowers

> Hint: Using fusible webbing only around edges of templates will help reduce bulk when layering each flower.

Making the Flowers

1. Using fusible webbing and pencil, draw around flower templates A, B and C onto dull side of webbing, keeping drawn flowers nestled inside each other.

2. Draw 13 nested flower templates A, B and C.

3. Cut out flower shapes. Cut 1/8" away from the solid line and carefully cut along dotted inner line of each template.

4. Place template A pieces on back of 8 ½" x 8 ½" squares, template B pieces on back of 6 ½" x 6 ½" squares and Template C pieces on back of 4 ½" x 4 ½" squares.

5. Carefully cut along the solid outer line of each template only. Do not cut along inner dotted line.

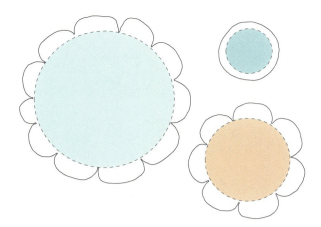

6. Following manufacturer's instructions, remove the paper and fuse the template piece to the fabric, making sure each template and fabric is lying flat before pressing.

Fusing the Flowers

1. Lay a large towel or blanket onto table or floor area (this is to allow for ironing flowers into place when ready). Lay quilt top over blanket or towel.

2. To make layout guide lines on quilt top, fold quilt in half lengthways and press fold line from top to bottom in middle of quilt top.

3. Open quilt. Fold each side into middle and press folded seam. These three pressed lines become guidelines for the placement of the flowers.

4. Lay all template A flowers onto quilt using pressed lines as a guide - in top row, lay template A to the left of line 1, the middle flower in the middle of line 2, and the third flower to the right of line 3.

5. In the second row, the first flower lays to the right of line 1 and the second flower lays to the left of line 3. Note, each flower sits in the centre of the three striped colour design, continue laying out template A flowers until happy with placement.

6. Using a glue stick, dab a couple of small spots of glue on back of each flower and press into place with fingers.

   Note: The position of the flower can be changed after glueing. Simply pull flower gently off quilt, reposition and re-glue.

7. Again referring to colour photo, place template B flowers centred onto centre of template A flowers until happy with placement. Dab a little glue under each template and press onto quilt with fingers. Repeat with template C circles. When finished placing all flower templates onto quilt, carefully fuse flowers into place.

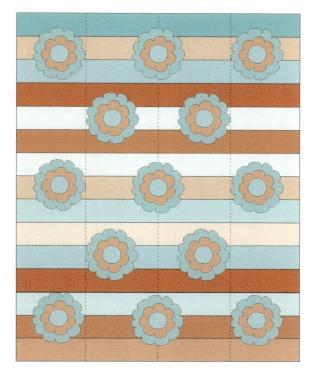

Borders

Border 1 (Green)

1. Cut 2 – 2 ½" x 42" strips. Attach to top and bottom of quilt.

2. Take 1 strip and cut in half to yield 2 – 2 ½" x 21" strips.

3. Using the remaining 2 - 2 ½" x 42" strips, sew a 2 ½" x 21" strip to each. Trim to 56 ½".

4. Attach to both sides of quilt top.

5. Press seams towards the border.

Border 2 (Cream)

1. Take one strip and cut in half to yield 2 – 2" x 21" strips.

2. Sew each 2 " x 21" strip onto 1 - 2" x 42" strip. Trim to 46".

3. Attach to top and bottom of quilt.

4. Take another strip and cut in half to yield 2 – 2" x 21" strips.

5. Using the remaining 2 - 2 ½" x 42" strips, sew a 2 ½" x 21" strip to each. Trim to 59 ½" inches.

6. Attach to both sides of quilt.

Backing

1. Join 2 – 13" x WOF strips together along short sides to make one long strip. Trim to 13" x 66"

2. Attach this strip to long side of the remaining 66 inches x WOF piece.

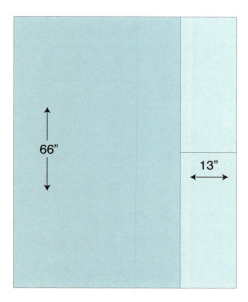

Quilting and Raw Edge Appliqué

The raw edge appliqué becomes part of the quilting that holds the three layers of the quilt together.

1. Lay quilt backing right side down onto table. Clip (or tape) in place.

2. Smooth wadding over backing, ensuring all sides are even.

3. Centre quilt top onto wadding and smooth from centre. Clip (or tape) in place.

4. Baste quilt sandwich with safety pins placed at 4" intervals.

5. Unclip from table.

Raw Edge Appliqué

1. Place darning foot into your machine as per sewing machine manual.

2. Lower the feed dogs (if feed dogs cannot lower put stitch length onto zero).

3. Raise your presser foot pressure if your machine allows it. Using a coloured thread (same colour top and bobbin) to match the appliqué colour, drop needle into edge of flower and lift up to bring bobbin thread to top of quilt.

4. Stitch two or three tiny securing stitches, then sew twice around edges of the flower. When nearing a safety pin, stop sewing, remove pin, resume sewing.

5. Finish with a couple of tiny securing stitches and cut threads.

6. Repeat sewing around every flower appliqué, changing thread colours to match fabric colour. Once all flowers have been appliquéd in place, quilt the remainder of quilt.

Note: if machine does not have darning foot, appliqué can be quilted into place using a walking foot. Different stitches can also be used such as buttonhole stitch, satin stitch or decorative stitch to secure appliqué templates onto quilt.

Finishing the Quilt.

Quilting

1. Quilt an overall design over the rest of the quilt. For example, using a tan or grey thread, quilt a medium sized meandering design (eg: stipple) over the quilt top and in between each flower. Cathy quilted her quilt using a curving zig zag stitch in a diamond design.

2. Bind and label the quilt.

Tips and Tricks

Raw edge appliqué/free motion quilting on domestic sewing machine

❀ Change machine needle before beginning a new quilt.

❀ Check posture - shoulders relaxed? Feet in comfortable position? Table at right height to sit comfortably at machine?

❀ Every 20 minutes or so, stop, take a few deep breaths, stand up and have a stretch, roll shoulders back down to relaxed position!

❀ **Raw edge appliqué** - it can help to wear quilters gloves. Relax, rest hands about 6 inches apart as a frame around appliqué. Gently move quilt around under the needle. Think of it like drawing on paper where the needle is the pencil. Stitch twice around edge of appliqué, this will ensure appliqué is well secured to quilt background. Raw edge appliqué will fray a little, adding interest to the design.

❀ **Free motion quilting** - before beginning a new FMQ design, it helps to draw design on paper first. This lets your brain know what you are wanting to do.

❀ If fused appliqué flowers begin to lift from quilt before quilting, use gluestick and dab a tiny amount of glue under lifted edge. Press appliqué onto quilt with fingers, ready to quilt.

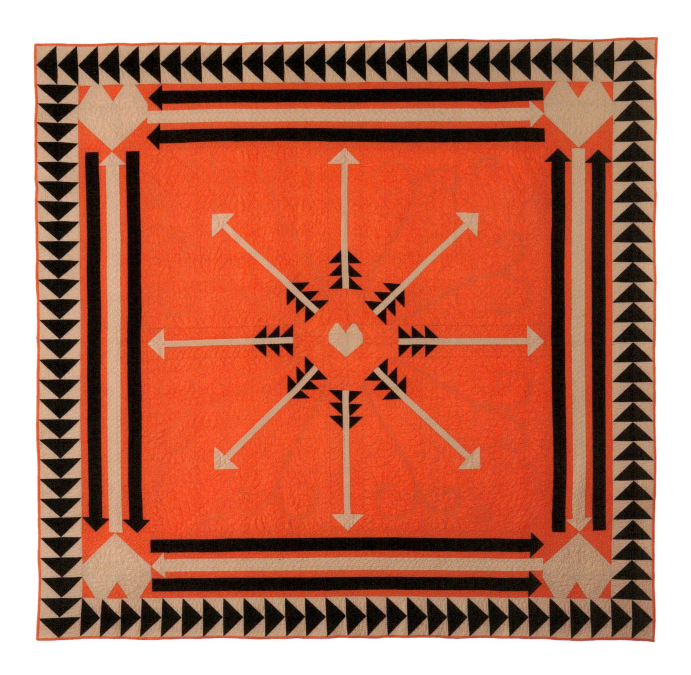

Arrow to the Heart

Charlotte Dumsney

Finished Quilt Size: 90" by 90" (2.3 m x 2.3 m)

Requirements

❀ Coral solid: 4 ½ yds (4 m)

❀ Pale pink solid: 3 yds (2.5 m)

❀ Black solid: 3 yds (2.5 m)

❀ Binding: 3/4 yd (0.75 m)

❀ Backing: 8.5 yds (8 m)

❀ Batting: 100" x 100" (2.5m x 2.5m)

Cutting

From the Coral solid cut:

Lengthwise from the yardage

✂ 4 - 23 ⅞" x 23 ⅞" squares. Cut once on the diagonal to yield 8 triangles (Piece E).

✂ 8 - 1 ½" x 56 ½" strips (Piece L).

✂ 8 - 1 ½" x 54 ½" strips (Piece M).

Across the width of fabric (WOF)

✂ 16 - 2 ½" x 13 ½" rectangle (Piece C).

✂ 4 - 5 ½" x 11 ½" rectangle (Piece H).

✂ 4 - 5 ½" x 5 ½" squares (Piece J).

✂ 24 - 2 ⅞" x 2 ⅞" squares (Piece A).

✂ 4 - 4 ⅜" x 4 ⅜" squares. Cut once on the diagonal to yield 8 triangles (Piece F).

✂ 8 - 3 ⅜" x 3 ⅜ " squares (Piece G).

✂ 12 - 2 ⅞" x 2 ⅞" squares (Piece N).

✂ 9 - 2" wide strips by WOF

From the Pale Pink solid cut:

Lengthwise from the yardage

✂ 4 - 2 ½" x 56 ½" strips (Piece Q).

✂ Across the width of fabric (WOF).

✂ 8 - 1 ½"x 19 ½" strips (Piece D).

✂ 2- 6 ½" x6 ½" squares (Piece I)

✂ 1 - 5 ¼" x 5 ¼" square (Piece O).

✂ 112 - 3 ⅞" x 3 ⅞" squares (Piece P).

From the Black solid cut:

Lengthwise from the yardage

✂ 8 x 2 ½" x 56 ½" strips (Piece K).

Across the width of fabric (WOF)

✂ 28 - 7 ¼" x 7 ¼"squares (Piece R).

✂ 2 - 5 ¼" x 5 ¼" squares (Piece S).

✂ 24 - 2 ⅞" x 2 ⅞"squares (Piece B).

Paper Piecing
Small heart cut:

Pale Pink

✂ 2 - 3 ½" x 2 ½" rectangles (A1, A5).

✂ 1 - 5 ½" x 4 ½" rectangle (A7).

Photographed by Charlotte Dumesny and Peter Condon Risk Studio Port Fairy

Cutting continued ......

Coral

- ✂ 2 - 3 ½" x 3" rectangles (A 8).
- ✂ 2 - 2 ½" x 2" rectangles (A2, A6).
- ✂ 1 - 3 x 2 ½" rectangle (A3).

Large hearts cut:

Pale Pink

- ✂ 8 - 4 ½ x 7 rectangles (A1, A5).
- ✂ 4 - 11 ½" x 7 ½" rectangles (A7).

Coral

- ✂ 8 - 6 ½" x 6" rectangles (A8).
- ✂ 8 - 4 ½" x 3 ½" rectangles (A2, A6).
- ✂ 4 - 4 ½" x 4" rectangles (A3).

Block Assembly

Centre Block

Making the Arrows

1. Draw a diagonal line from corner to corner on wrong side of fabric of Piece A. Repeat for remaining 23 pieces.

2. Place Piece A right sides together on Piece B.

3. Sew ¼" seam on each side of the marked line.

4. Cut along line and press blocks open to yield 48 Half Square Triangles (HST).

5. Sew 3 HST together to make a vertical strip.

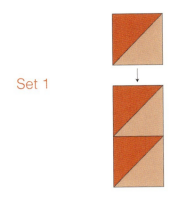

Set 1

6. Sew 3 more HST's together, this time flipping HST blocks.

Set 2

7. Make 8 of each HST set.

8. Using Piece C, sew to top of each set of HST's. Make 16.

9. Sew Piece D in centre.

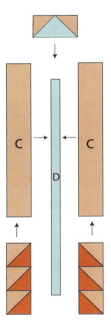

10. Make 8 flying geese using Pieces G and I. (See 'Making the flying geese'). Sew each of the flying geese to the top of the long rectangular blocks to give you 8 arrow blocks.

11. Take 4 of the arrow blocks and sew Piece H to the top of each.

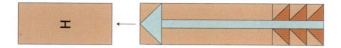

12. Sew Piece E to either side of arrow.

13. Sew Piece F to both the top and bottom corner of the large block to produce 4 large square blocks.

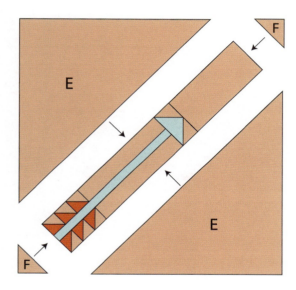

14. Sew Piece J to the bottom of each of the 4 remaining arrow blocks .

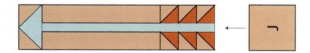

15. Layout the finished blocks and sew together.

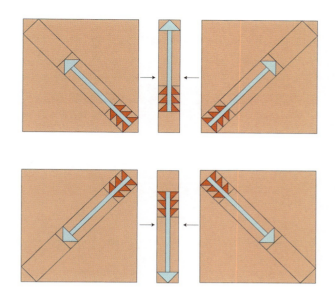

16. Repeat the above 2 steps for the remaining 2 large arrow blocks.

17. Make 1 small heart using template A.

18. Using the remaining 2 arrow blocks, sew one to the left hand side of the heart and one to the right hand side of the heart, ensuring that both arrows are pointing outwards.

19. Sew the centre block together.

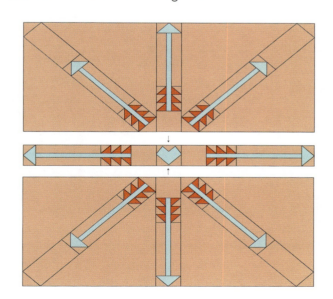

Border 1 (Arrows)

1. Sew Piece L to the top of each Piece K. Repeat 3 more times to yield 4 strips.

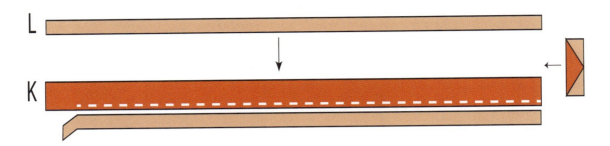

2. Sew Piece M to the bottom of each strip, lining it up so it is flush with the left hand side, stopping 2" before the end (partial seam) .

3. Sew Piece L to the bottom of each Piece K. Repeat 3 more times to yield 4 strips.

4. Sew Piece M to the top of each strip, lining it up so it is flush with the left hand side, stopping 2" before the end (partial seam).

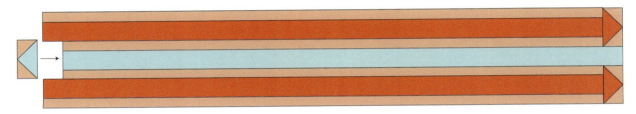

5. Using Piece S, Piece O, and Piece N, make 12 flying geese, 8 black and 4 pale pink. (See 'Making the flying geese').

6. Sew the black flying geese to the straight end of the black and coral strip blocks.

7. Sew 2 arrow strips to Piece Q.

8. Repeat the above step for the other 3 long arrow borders.

9. Using the pale pink flying geese arrowheads, sew to centre 3 strips.

10. Complete the partial seams that had been left earlier.

11. Repeat for the other three border blocks.

12. Sew 4 large paper pieced heart blocks using Template B.

Border 2 (Flying Geese)

1. Using Piece R and Piece P, make 112 flying geese. (See 'Making the flying geese').

2. Sew 2 strips of 26 blocks and 2 strips of 28 blocks. Make sure they are facing the same direction.

3. Place the remaining 4 to one side.

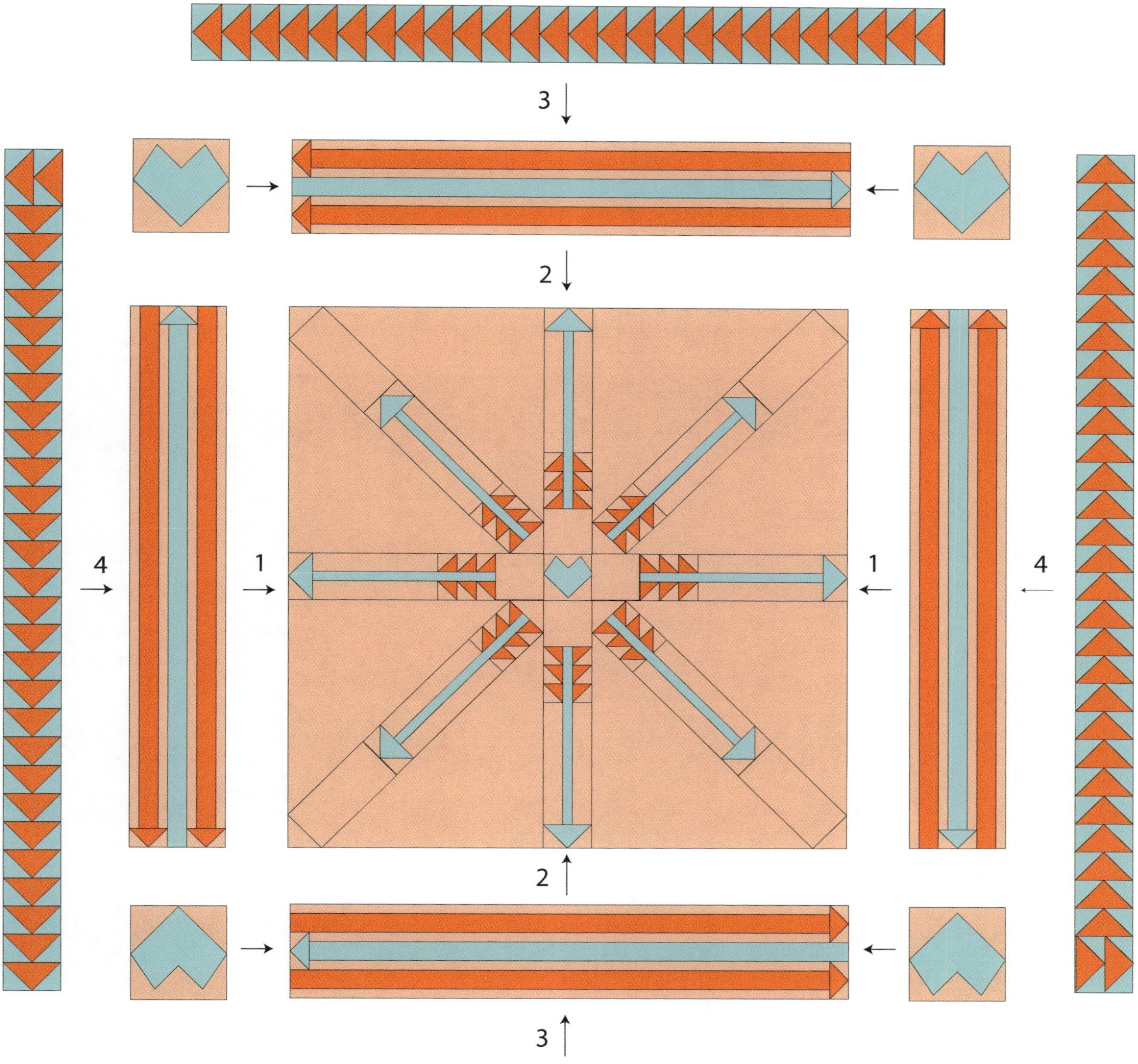
3
2
4
1
1
4
2
3

Quilt Assembly

Borders

Note: Each border is rotated in the opposite direction to each other.

1. Sew an arrow border to the top and bottom of the finished centre block. Sew 4 large hearts on either end of the 2 arrow borders.

2. Sew an arrow border with large hearts to both sides.

3. Sew a 26 - block flying geese border to the top and bottom of the quilt.

4. Take the remaining 4 flying geese blocks and sew together into two pairs, facing the same direction.

5. Sew one pair each to the top end of a 28 – block strip, ensuring the 28 -blocks are facing down and the pair of geese blocks are facing left.

6. Add 30 block flying geese border to each side, rotating the right hand border so the geese blocks are facing up and the pair of geese blocks are facing right.

Finishing the Quilt

1. Prepare the backing.

2. Baste, quilt and bind your quilt.

Arrow to the Heart was quilted by Yvonne McRae at Allambi Quiltery.

Making the Flying Geese

1. Select 1 background square (large square) and 4 squares for triangle pieces (small squares). Draw a line diagonally from one corner to another on the 4 small squares.

2. Place 2 small squares, right sides together, on opposite corners of the large square. Sew scant ¼" either side of the drawn line. Press the unit to set seams.

3. Cut along the line. Press open to create 2 heart shape units.

4. Place remaining 2 small squares on heart shape units so the small square is on top of the background square and draw a diagonal line from the bottom corner up into the centre. Sew scant ¼" on either side of line. Press unit to set seams.

5. Cut along line and press open to give 8 flying geese blocks.

6. Trim flying geese blocks if required.

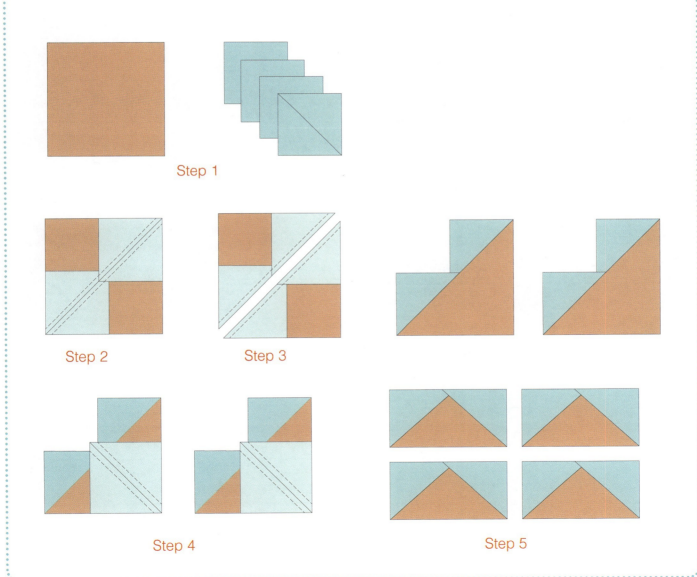

Step 1

Step 2

Step 3

Step 4

Step 5

Rachaeldaisy

Finished Block Size 7" x 7" (17.5 cm)

Finished Quilt Size 56" x 56" (1.4 m x 1.4 m)

Requirements

- Background fabrics: 7 ½" (18.75 cm) x WOF each of 13 assorted dark background fabrics

- Melon Fabrics:40 – 9 ½"x 4 ½" (23.75 cm x 11.25 cm)

- Ric-rac: A total of 12 ½ yards (11m) of 1" Ric-rac. 2 ½ yards (2 ½ m) each of 5 colours

- Yo-Yo fabric: 24 - 5"x 5"squares (12.5 cm x 12.5 cm) of different bright fabrics

- Binding fabric: 6 - 40" x 2 ½'" wide strips (6.25 cm x 100 cm), 3 black and 3 other colours

- Backing Fabric: 3 ½ yards (3.2 m)

- Batting: 62" x 62" (1.6 m x 1.6 m)

- Template plastic or freezer paper - 10" x 15" (25cm x 37.5 cm)

- Matching thread

- Rotary cutter, scissors, cutting mat, rulers

Cutting

Assorted dark background fabric

- Cut 13 – 7 ½" x WOF strips.

- Cut 64 - 7 ½" x 7 ½" squares.

Melon fabric

- Using the template plastic, make template A and B.

- Trace onto fabric and cut out melon shapes on the line.

- Cut 36 centre melons using template A.

- Cut 4 Edge Melons using template B.

Binding fabric

- Cut 3 - 2 ½" x WOF strips of assorted dark fabrics.

- Cut 1 each – 2 ½" x WOF strips of 3 coloured fabrics.

Yo-Yos

- Use template C to make circles out of template plastic or freezer paper. Use template to cut out 24 circles.

Photography by Phil Dodd and Rachaeldaisy

Block Assembly

1. Place your dark assorted background squares randomly into 8 rows of 8. Move them around until you are pleased with the layout. Refer to photo of quilt for colour placement.

2. Rest melon shapes on the background squares to make sure you're happy with your fabric choices. If a melon doesn't look right it's better to change before wasting rac-rac on a melon you won't use.

Centre Block

Hint: The ric-rac can be sewn using one long piece. To chain piece simply line up another melon shape on the ric-rac and sew. Cut the pieces apart when finished.

1. Starting at one end of the melon, lay ric-rac onto the fabric right side up.

2. Line up the rac-rac so that centre of the rac-rac is in on the ¼ inch line of the fabric.

3. It is important that you sew on the inside of the "valleys" of the ric-rac. Sew along ¼ inch from the edge of the fabric. There's no need to pin the rac-rac onto the fabric, just line it up along the edge as you slowly sew. When you reach the end, trim the rac-rac and repeat on other edge.

4. Trim rac-rac, and repeat on the opposite edge

5. Using an iron, press the melon piece on the wrong side of fabric to set the stitches.

Note: As most ric-rac trims are polyester, don't forget to use a cooler setting or a pressing cloth when using your iron.

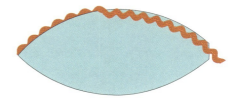

6. Fold the rac-rac along the sewn lines so that half of the rac-rac goes to the back and half remains at the front, press well.

7. Place melon shape into position on top of black background square.

8. Press to ensure flat and pin into place.

9. Using matching thread, stitch as close to edge of folded edge of melon for a neat look. This completes 1 block.

Hint: The scruffy ends of the ric-rac will be hidden later by yo-yos so there's no need to worry about them.

Edge Block

The melons at the edge of the quilt have continuous rac-rac around the point that will be closest to the binding.

1. Starting at the flat end, as per previous centre melons, sew rac-rac on right side of fabric, until ¼" from pointed end.
Don't cut ric-rac yet.

2. Press sewn side of rac-rac open. With fabric right side up fold rac-rac over the point and sew along the other edge.

3. Open out rac-rac and press well.

4. Sew to background fabric.

Quilt Assembly

Sew blocks carefully together, tucking protruding ric-rac edges out of the way as you sew. Rather than sewing into rows, sew the squares into four to make sure the corners line up then sew those squares into rows.

Finishing the Quilt

Backing

1. Cut fabric into 2 lengths of 63".

2. Remove selvedges and sew together or make a pieced backing from pieces of fabric to equal a size of 63" square.

> Hint: I like to pin or masking tape an outline of the required size on a design wall or floor and then place fabrics within the marked area with fabrics into a pleasing layout. When happy with the results sew together to make backing.

Quilting

This quilt was quilted in the ditch around the background squares and then diagonally across the quilt in wavy lines to quilt around the melons. I also added some hand quilted big stitches in perle 8 thread in melon shapes on some of the squares.

Yo-Yos

1. Fold a ¼ inch hem to the wrong side of the fabric and secure with a couple of back stitches.

2. Sew with a generous ¼ " running stitch close to the edge of the circle, continuing to fold a ¼" seam inwards as you go.

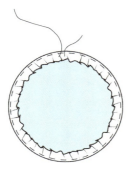

3. Pull thread tightly (but try not to break it) and gather the top with right side of fabric on the outside.

4. Shape into a Yo-Yo and pull thread to the back, tie off and knot. Appliqué the Yo-Yos into position.

Hint: Try to finish with the needle going through/near the hole you started with in the same direction.

Binding

1. It's fun to add a bit of colour to the binding. To decide where to have the strips of colour, lay them along the sides of the quilt.

2. When happy with the approximate positions of the colours placed between the darker binding fabrics, pin the strips together lengthwise in order.

3. Sew binding using your favourite method and attach to the quilt.

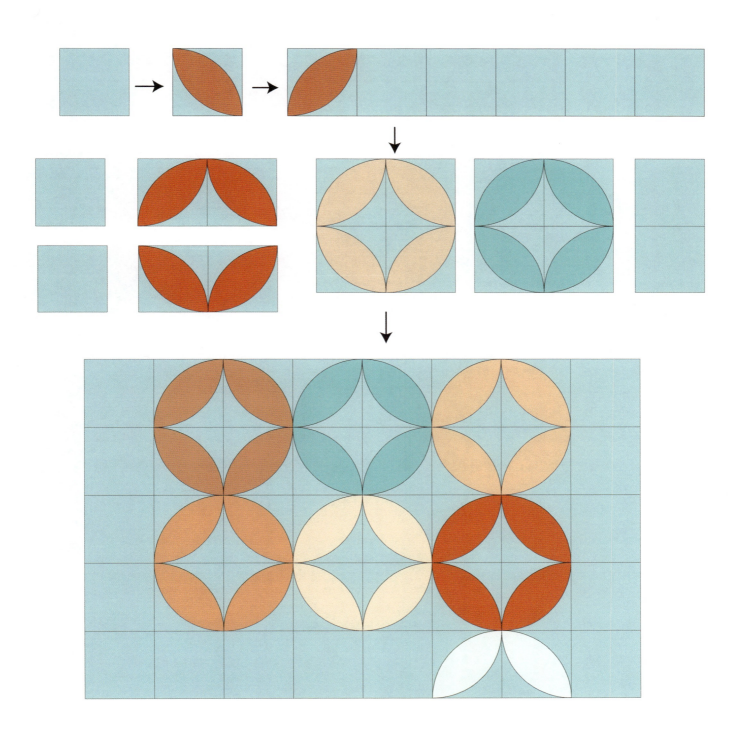

Rock Pools

Jane Davidson

Finished Block Size: 20" x 20" (51 cm x 51 cm)

Finished Quilt Size: 85" x 85" (2.15 m x 2.15 m)

Requirements

Width of Fabric (WOF) calculated at 42"

- ❀ 35 fat quarters of assorted fabrics.

- ❀ Background 1 - 9 ½ yds (9 m)

  Note: 2 – 20 ½" x 20 ½" squares can be cut across the Width of Fabric (WOF) with selvages removed from a 44" wide fabric. If the fabric is less than 42", with selvages removed, then 12 yards of fabric will be required.

- ❀ Background 2 - 3 yds (2.74 m)

- ❀ Stems: 1 - fat eighth of orange print

- ❀ Binding - ¾" yds (70 cms)

- ❀ Backing fabric - 5 ½" yds (5.1 m)

- ❀ Batting - 93"x 93" (2.4 m x 2.4 m)

- ❀ Template plastic - ¼ grid markings

- ❀ Freezer paper

- ❀ Erasable marking pen or chalk pencil

- ❀ Dresden ruler/template

  The Dresden blades are all cut using template A. As an alternative to making your own template, any 12" - 30 degree Dresden ruler can be used. Use the 9" marking on the ruler as the unfinished height of the blade.

Template Preparation

1. Trace templates A, B, C, D and E onto template plastic.

2. Cut on solid line.

3. Make 1 of each.

Cutting

From background 1 fabric cut:

- ✂ 13 - 20 ½"x 20 ½" squares for Dresden blocks.

- ✂ 3 - 3 ¾" x WOF strips. Cut into 78 - 1 ½" x 3 ¾" rectangles (Row 1).

- ✂ 2 – 5 ½" x WOF strips. Cut into 78 - 1" x 5 ½" rectangles (Row 3).

- ✂ 2 – 7 ½" x WOF strips. Cut into 78 - 1" x 7 ½" rectangles (Row 5).

- ✂ 2 – 8" x WOF strips. Cut into 78 - 1" x 8" rectangles (Row 7).

- ✂ 5 – 4 ½" x WOF strips. Cut into 39 - 4 ½" x 4 ½" squares. Cut once on the diagonal to yield 78 triangles (Row 9).

- ✂ 24 – 3" x 10" rectangles (Piece B).

- ✂ 12 – 1 ½" x 10" rectangles (Piece D).

- ✂ 25 – 4" x 10" rectangles (Piece E).

- ✂ 13 – 2 ¼" x 10" rectangles (Piece G).

- ✂ 16 – 4 ½" x 10" rectangles (Piece H).

- ✂ 16 – 2 ¾" x 10" rectangles (Piece J).

- ✂ Trace the circle template B onto back of fabric. Cut 13 circles. Add ¼" seam allowance for hand turned appliqué.

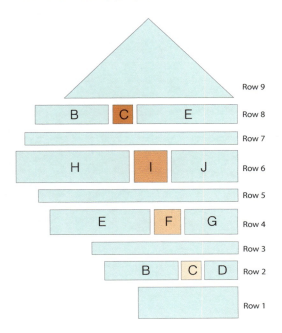

Cutting continued ....

From background 2 Fabric cut:

✂ 2 - 15" x 15" squares. Cut once on the diagonal to yield 4 corner triangles.

✂ 2 - 29 ½" x 29 ½" squares. Cut diagonally twice to yield 8 Setting triangles.

✂ 5 – 5 ½" x WOF strips. Cut into 56 – 3 ¼" x 5 ½" rectangles (Piece K).

✂ 3 – 6 ½" x WOF strips. Cut into 28 – 4 ¼" x 6 ½" rectangles (Piece M).

✂ Trace 8 template C onto back of fabric. Cut 8 half circles. Add ¼" seam allowance for hand turned appliqué.

✂ Trace 4 template D onto back of fabric. Cut 4 quarter circles. Add ¼" seam allowance for hand turned appliqué.

From assorted fat quarters cut:

✂ 204 – 3 ½" x 10" rectangles (Piece A).

✂ 24 - 1 ¼" x 10" strips (Piece C).

✂ 13 - 1 ½" x 10" strips (Piece F).

✂ 16 - 1 ¾" x 10" strips (Piece I).

✂ 16 - 3 ¼" x 9" rectangles (Piece N).

✂ 28 – 2 ¼" x 4 ½" rectangles (Piece O).

From stem fabric cut:

✂ 28 – 1" x 5 ½" rectangles (Piece L).

From binding fabric cut:

✂ 9 - 2 ½" x WOF strips for double-fold binding.

Photography by Linda Riordan and Antoinette O'Sullivan

Quilting by Jane Davidson

Making a Dresden Wedge

1. Fold each blade right sides together.

2. Sew ¼" from top. Trim excess from folded corner.

3. Fold open and turn right side out. Use a pointed tool to push out tip. The tip should be in-line with the centre.

4. Press blade.

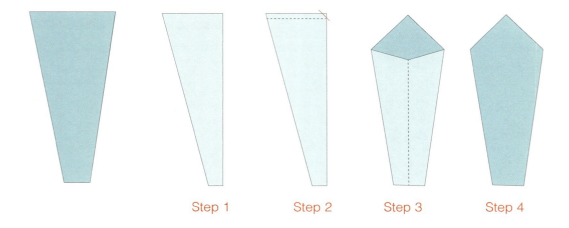

Step 1   Step 2   Step 3   Step 4

Block Assembly

All seam allowances are ¼".

Blade A:

1. Select 102 contrasting pairs of 3 ½" x 10" strips of assorted fabrics (Piece A).

2. Sew them together lengthways. Press seams to one side. Make 102.

3. Using template A, place centre registration line on seam and cut out blade.

4. Make 102 solid blades.

(See Making a Dresden Wedge)

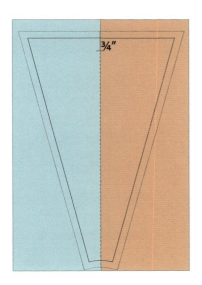

Blade B (pieced)

Strip sets are made and cut into pieces for Blade B. Press all seams open.

Set 1:

1. Join Pieces B, C and D lengthwise.

2. Make 12.

3. Cut 7 – 1 ¼" strips from each block to yield 78 (Row 2).

Set 2:

1. Join pieces E, F and G lengthwise.

2. Make 13.

3. Cut 6 – 1 ½" strips from each block to yield 78 (Row 4).

Set 3:

1. Join pieces H, I and J lengthwise.

2. Make 16.

3. Cut 5 – 1 ¾" strips from each block to yield 78 (Row 6).

Set 4:

1. Join pieces B, C an E lengthwise.

2. Make 12.

3. Cut 7 – 1 ¼" strips from each block to yield 78 (Row 8).

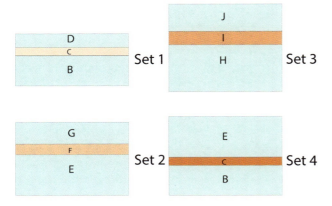

Assemble Blade B

1. Assemble the pieced blade B in groups and then join the groups. Rows 1 – 8 are staggered from the right hand side. Row 9 is staggered from the left hand side.

2. Press all seams away from the pieced strips. Use the Blade B layout diagram as a reference while assembling the blade.

> Hint: Use a small 1" x 6" ruler to measure the staggers or cut a small piece of ¼" marked template plastic 1 ¼" x 1 ¼" square to use a guide for staggering the rows.

Section 1:

1. Lay out rows 1, 2 and 3.

2. Begin row 2, ½" in from Row 1.

3. Begin row 3, flush with Row 2.

Section 2:

4. Lay out rows 4 and 5.

5. Begin row 5, ½" in from Row 4.

Section 3:

6. Lay out rows 6 and 7.

7. Begin row 7, ½" in from row 6.

Section 4:

8. Lay out row 8 and 9.

9. Begin row 9, 1 ¼" in from row 8, starting from the left.

10. Sew Groups 1 – 4 together. Stagger each group set by ½". This will be the measurement between the pieced squares in each section.

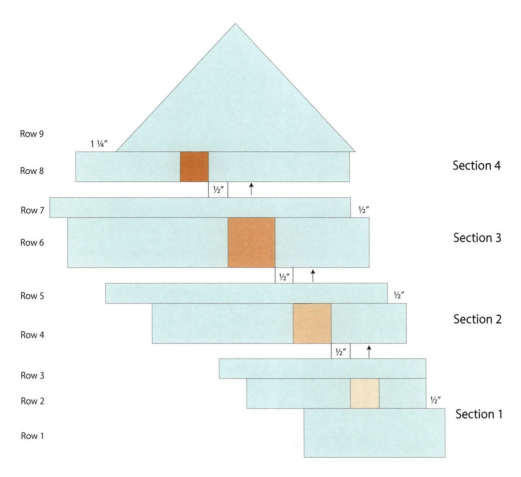

11. Place the template A on the right side of the pieced blade and align the top ¾'' mark at with the top of the pieced square in row 8. Place centre line running through the centre of all 4 pieced squares.

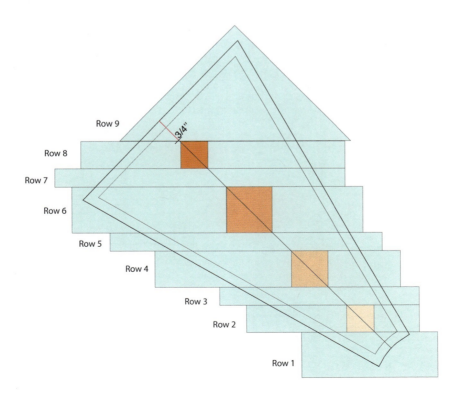

12. Trim carefully around template.

13. Make blade as per instructions, *Making a Dresden Wedge.*

14. Make 78 blades.

Note: By request, those who prefer paper piecing, an optional paper piecing template is available in the 'Templates' section of the publication. Fabric and cutting requirements will differ from pattern and are not included in this publication.

Blade C (Anemone)

1. Sew Piece K on either side of Piece L. Press seams away from Piece L.

2. Sew Piece M on top.

3. Place template A so centre line is middle of Piece L and base is touching bottom edge of block.

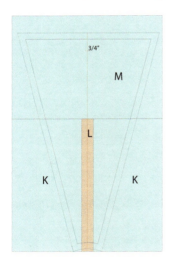

4. Cut 28 blades. Make blade as per instructions for Blade A.

5. Make 28.

Half Blades

1. Using template A, place the centre marking ¼" in from right edge on Piece N. Cut half a wedge.

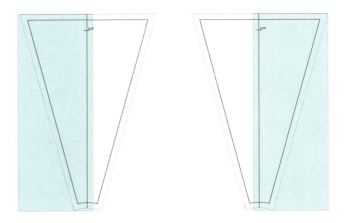

2. Fold down corner to wrong side and press into place.

3. Repeat for left side.

4. Make 16.

Preparation of Appliqué Full Circles (Template B).

1. Trace template B into dull side of freezer paper. Cut out on line.

2. Press shiny side of freezer paper to wrong side of circle.

3. Press seam allowance around edge of back of freezer paper, pulling firmly so no pleating occurs.

4. Starch circle and gently remove freezer paper. Use the creased edge as a guide when appliquéing piece to block.

5. Make 13.

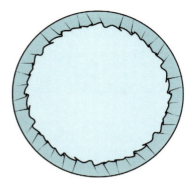

Half Circle (Template C).

1. Use same technique as for *Full Circles.* Do not press the ¼" seam along the straight edge over the back of the freezer paper template. This will be sewn into the seam.

2. Make 8.

Quarter Circle (Template D).

1. Use same technique as for *Full Circles.* Do not press the ¼" seam along the two straight edges over the back of the freezer paper template. These will be sewn into the seam.

2. Make 4.

Anemone (Template E).

1. Trace template E into dull side of freezer paper. Cut out on line.

2. Press shiny side of freezer paper to wrong side of Piece O. Cut around template leaving a ¼" seam allowance.

3. Press seam allowance around edge on back freezer paper, pulling firmly so no pleating occurs.

4. Starch piece and gently remove freezer paper. Use the creased edge as a guide when appliquéing piece to block.

5. Appliqué template E on to Blade C. Place the shape ¼" from top of blade. Cover top of stem.

6. Make 28.

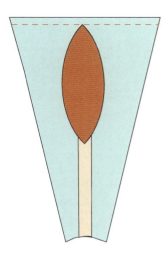

Assembly

Centre Setting Blocks – Full Dresden Block

1. Group 6 Blade A and 6 Blade B into 13 piles.

2. Sew the blades together in pairs of Blade A and Blade B.

3. Join the pairs to make a half a Dresden plate.

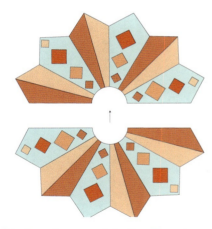

4. Join 2 halves to complete the Dresden plate.

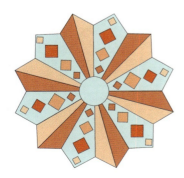

5. Press seams away from Blade B.

6. Appliqué the circles to the centre of the block.

7. Fold a 20 ½" x 20 ½" background square into 4 and finger press. Fold again diagonally and finger press.

8. Align the block with the fold marks.

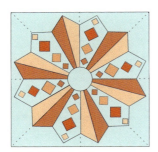

9. Appliqué to background square.

10. Cut away excess background fabric, leaving a ¼" seam allowance.

Border Setting Blocks – Half Dresden Blocks

1. Sew Blade A, Blade C and 2 half blades together.

2. Take a setting triangle and press in half.

3. Position the Half Dresden Block on the triangle, using the centre fold mark as a guide. Appliqué the Half Dresden Block to setting triangle.

4. Appliqué Half circle to the block.

5. Cut away excess background fabric, leaving a ¼" seam allowance.

6. Make 8.

Corner Setting Blocks (Quarter Dresden Blocks)

1. Sew a Blade A on either side of a Blade C.

2. Take a corner setting triangle and press in half.

3. Position the Quarter Dresden Block on the corner triangle, using the centre fold mark as a guide.

4. Appliqué Quarter Dresden Block to the corner setting triangle

5. Cut away excess background fabric, leaving a ¼" seam allowance.

6. Make 4.

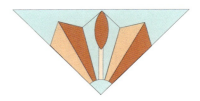

Quilt Assembly

1. Sew diagonal rows together, leaving the 4 corner blocks to be attached after the body of the quilt has been completed.

2. Press seams open.

> Hint: The setting and corner triangles are cut on the bias. Handling block carefully and stabilizing fabric with a stay stitch is recommended.

Quilting and Finishing

1. Cut backing fabric in half to yield 2 - 2 ¾ yard pieces. Remove selvages.

2. Piece an 8" x 99" wide strip from left over assorted fat quarter fabrics and background solid pieces.

3. Sew the three sections together with pieced strip in the middle.

4. Layer and baste the quilt. Quilt as desired.

5. Bind the quilt.

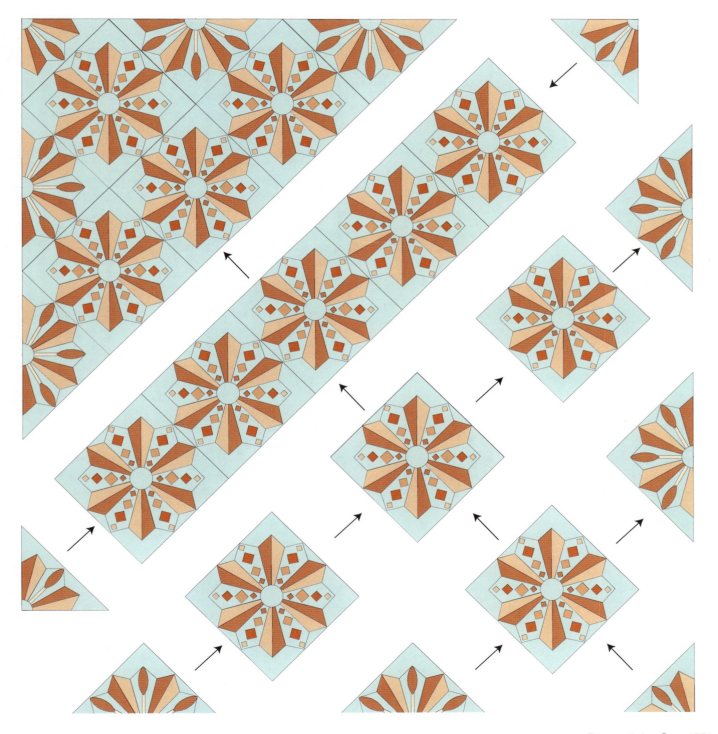

Jeannette Bruce

Finished Block Size: 6" x 6" (15.2 cm x 15.2 cm)

Finished Quilt Size: 71" x 85" (1.8 m x 2.08 m)

Requirements

This is a scrappy quilt where each block is made using an unique set of fabrics.

- 🌼 ⅓ yd each of 25 assorted prints
- 🌼 50 fat eighths of assorted solid fabrics
- 🌼 Black text print: 2 yds (2 m)
- 🌼 Striped corner sashing : ¼ yd (25 cm)
- 🌼 Binding: 1 ¼" yards (1.2 m) of binding fabric
- 🌼 Backing: 5 ¼" yds (5 m)
- 🌼 Batting : 78" x 93" (1.9 m x 2.4 m)
- 🌼 6 ½" x 6 ½" square ruler
- 🌼 Lightweight fusible webbing (17" or 43 cm wide) – 4 ¼ yards (3.9 m) for appliqué
- 🌼 Pencil / marking pen

Cutting

X – Blocks

From each of the assorted prints cut:

- ✂ 2 - 5" x 5" squares (Piece A).
- ✂ 1 – 2 ½" x 2 ½" squares (Piece B).
- ✂ 1 – 1 ½" x 1 ½" squares (Piece C).

From each of the 50 fat eighths of solid fabrics cut:

- ✂ 1 - 1 ½" x 10" rectangles (Piece D).
- ✂ 2 – 1 ½" x 5" rectangles (Piece E).

Place each group of pieces into 50 separate piles.

O – Blocks

From each of the assorted prints cut:

- ✂ 2 – 3" x 6" rectangles. Cut into 2 – 3" x 3" squares. Keep pairs together. (Piece F).
- ✂ 2 – 2" x 4 ½" rectangles (Piece G).
- ✂ 2 – 2" x 7 ½" rectangles (Piece H).

From each of the 50 fat eighths of solid fabrics cut:

- ✂ 1 – 6" x 6" squares (Piece I).

Place each group of pieces into 49 separate piles.

Sashing and Border

From the striped corner sashing fabric cut:

- ✂ 5 – 1 ½" x WOF strips.
  Cut 120 – 1 ½" x 1 ½" squares. (Piece J).

From the black text print cut:

- ✂ 42 – 1 ½" x WOF strips. From these strips cut 218 – 1 ½" x 6 ½" rectangles (Piece K) and 42 – 1 ½" x 4 ½" rectangles (Piece L).

From each of the 50 fat eighths of solid fabrics cut:

- ✂ 3 - 2 ½" x 4 ½" rectangles (Piece M).

Corner border squares cut:

- ✂ 4 – 4" x 4" squares (Piece N).

Quilted and Photographed by Jeannette Bruce

Block Assembly

X – Block

1. Select 2 – 5" x 5" squares (Piece A) that contrasts well with each other. Cut each square into 4 – 2 ½" x 2 ½" squares. Make 50 sets.

2. Select 1- 2 ½" x 2 ½"square (Piece B) that contrasts well with two fabrics and add to pile.

3. Assemble the 9-patch block. Place Piece B in the centre of row 2.

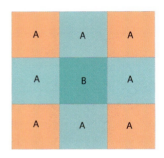

4. Sew the squares into three rows. Press the top and bottom rows towards the outside. Press the middle row towards the centre fabric.

5. Sew the rows together to create the 9-patch block and press the rows towards the outside. Make 50.

6. Select one 1 ½" x 1 ½" square (Piece C) and contrasting 2 – 1 ½" x 5" rectangles (Piece E).

7. Sew Piece E to either end of Piece C. Press the seams to the outside. Make 50.

8. Place each finished piece with the 9-patch, remembering to choose solids that show contrast to the 9-patch blocks.

9. Add a matching solid 1 ½" x 10" (Piece D) to each pile.

10. For each 9-patch block, make a diagonal cut from one corner to the opposite corner.

11. Finger press each of the 9-patch pieces down the centre.

12. Finger press Piece D in half.

13. Sew the 1 ½" x 10" (Piece D) solid segment to one half of divided 9-patch piece. Line up the centre fold marks. It is important to make sure to leave a little of the solid fabric overhanging over the edge of each end past the nine patch unit.

14. Sew the other half of the divided 9-patch to the centre strip. Line up the centre fold marks.

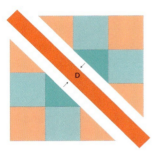

15. Press the seams towards the centre.

16. Diagonally cut a slice across the opposite corners to the centre strip.

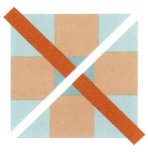

17. Fold the two pieces in half and finger press.

18. Sew the matching pieced centre strip to one half. Line them up so that the centre square is exactly in the middle. The seam allowances should be in opposing directions, place a pin at each join and sew one side at a time. Press the seams towards the centre.

19. Sew the other half to the pieced centre strip.

20. Using the 6 ½ inch square ruler, square up each block. Take time with this process and make sure that the corners are as centred as possible. It is helpful to have a ruler that has diagonal lines to help in the squaring up process.

21. Make 50.

O - Blocks:

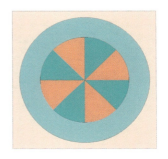

Centre pinwheels

1. Select from 3" x 3" squares (Piece F), 2 pairs of contrasting squares. Place to one side in 49 piles.

2. From each pile, select 1 pair of squares and draw a diagonal line from corner to corner on the back of one pair of 3" squares.

3. Place the contrasting 3" x 3" squares right sides together.

4. Using the chain piecing method of sewing, sew a very scant ¼" to the right of each side of the drawn lines.

5. Sew all pairs together.

6. Cut along the drawn line. Press the seams toward the darker fabric.

7. Make 4 – half square triangles (HST) from each two pair set.

8. Using the 6 ½" ruler, square each half square triangle (HST) to 2 ½" x 2 ½" square.

9. Arrange the 4 - half square triangles (HST) into the pinwheel layout.

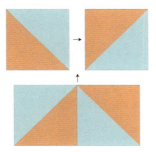

10. Sew each unit one at a time, making sure to press all seams in opposite directions.

11. Once the unit has been sewed and pressed, remove a couple of stitches on the reverse side where the seams cross over. This will allow the centre seam mini pinwheel to become free and can be pressed from the reverse side to allow the seams to all lie flat.

12. Make 49 pinwheels.

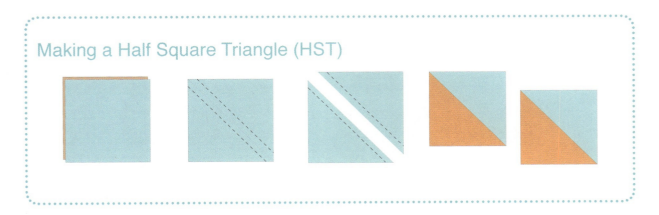

Making a Half Square Triangle (HST)

13. Select 2 – 2" x 4 ½" rectangles (Piece G) and 2 - 2" x 7 ½" (Piece H) from the same fabric to complement the 49 pinwheel units. There should be two extra backgrounds; use these to help in case of error or should more choice be needed in creating contrast.

14. Place in 49 piles.

15. Using the chain piecing method of sewing, sew in order, Piece G to the sides of one pinwheel block and then Piece H to the top and bottom of the pinwheel block. Press seams to the outside.

    Note: The block will measure 7 ½" x 7 ½" square. The block will be trimmed back after the appliqué is completed.

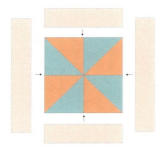

16. Following the manufacturer's instructions, fuse one 6" x 6" square of fusible webbing to the wrong side of a 6" x 6" square (Piece I).

17. For each square, make a X in the middle by folding in quarters and finger pressing to make a crease.

18. On the full side of the fusible webbing ironed to each square, line up the centre of the 5 ½" circle (template A), placing the centre of the circle in the centre of the folded lines.

19. Using a pencil, draw a line around the outside of the template

20. On the same square, line up the centre of the 3 ½" circle (template B), placing the centre of the circle in the centre of the folder lines.

21. Draw around the outside of the template.

22. Using a pair of sharp scissors, cut out each circle on the pencil line. Make 49 'O's.

23. Select a contrasting 'O' shape to complement each pinwheel block.

24. Remove the paper from the fusible webbing and carefully place over the pinwheels making sure to cover each corner exactly. Repeat for each of the 49 blocks.

25. Using your preferred stitch, machine appliqué each block.

26. Square each block keeping the 'O' centred.

Quilt Assembly

Hint: Arrange the quilt according to colour so that like colours are next to one another moving from warm colours at the top of the quilt to cool colours towards the bottom. This creates a wash effect. Alternatively, randomly place the blocks for a completely different look.

Sashing

1. Sew 1 - 1 ½" x 6 ½" rectangle (Piece K) to the top of each of the 99 'X' and 'O' blocks. Press the seams towards the outside.

2. Sew the 1 ½" x 1 ½" square (Piece J) to the 1 ½" x 6 ½" rectangles (Piece L) and press the seams towards the square.

3. Add the finished pieced sashing strips to the sides of all 99 'X' and 'O' blocks. Press the seams towards the outside.

4. Using a large design wall, arrange the blocks into 11 rows of 9 starting with an 'X' block at the top left and alternating O's with X's until all 99 blocks are laid out. Continue arranging until a pleasing effect is achieved.

5. Once all the blocks have been arranged, sew the remaining 20 pieced sashing strips to the left side of the 11 blocks on the left side of the quilt. Sew 9 strips to the bottom of the blocks on the bottom row. Press the seams towards the outside.

6. Sew the blocks into rows, one at a time. Press the seams to one side on the first row and alternate the direction the next row so that the seam rows are opposing each other

7. Sew the rows together taking care to pin at each seam and removing pins before sewing over them. Press the seams to the side. Press the top well from the front side.

Borders

Note: The scalloped borders will be cut once the quilting has been completed.

1. Sew 3 - 2 ½" x 4 ½" rectangles (Piece M) together to create 40 sets. Press the seams open.

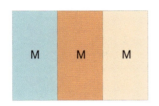

Top and Bottom Borders

1. Sew 10 - 1 ½" x 4 ½" rectangles (Piece L) to each end of 9 sets. Make 2.

2. Add 2 - 4 ½" x 4 ½" squares (Piece N) to the ends of each of the two rows. Press the seams open.

Side Borders

1. Sew 10 - 1 ½" x 4 ½" rectangles (Piece L) to each end of 11 sets. Press the seams open. Make 2.

Adding borders

1. Match the seams of the quilt with the side borders and sew. Press the seams towards the outside. Match the seams of the top and bottom borders and sew. Press the seams towards the outside.

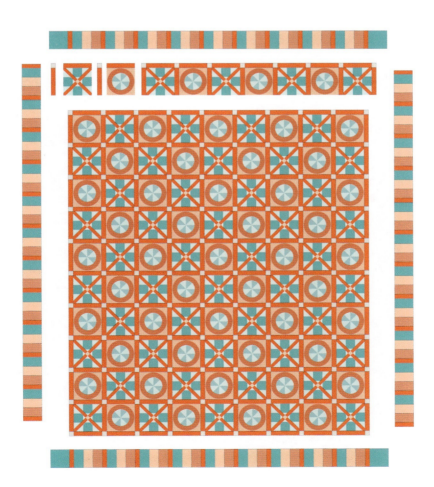

Finishing the Quilt

The quilt top is quilted before the edges are scalloped and bound.

1. Layer, baste and quilt as desired.

Scalloped Border

1. Using the 7 ½" half circle (template C), line up the straight edge of the template along one of the edges.

2. With a marking pen, draw a line along the curved outside edge of the template.

3. Continue repositioning the template C, lining up along the edge of the quilt and creating half circles along all four sides of the quilt.

Binding

1. Make 2 ½" x 385" of continuous, double fold bias binding.

2. Attach the binding by starting three quarters of the way along a scallop leaving about a 5" tail.

3. Using the drawn line as a guide, sew a ¼" seam allowance stopping at each inside corner, pivoting, rearranging the fabric by folding up and back in the same manner corner edges are treated on square edged quilts.

4. Continue sewing on the drawn scalloped line around the entire quilt until the last scallop is reached. Stop about one third of the way along the starting scallop and leave the leftover binding.

5. Using fabric scissors cut a ¼" beyond the drawn line to allow for fill within the binding.

6. Carefully cut around the entire quilt.

7. Lay the quilt flat and overlap the two tail ends in the middle of the scallop.

8. Cut the tails so that exactly 2 ½" are overlapping each other.

9. Sew the 2 ends rights sides together at a 45° angle.

10. Trim the seam to ¼" and finger press the seam open.

11. Pin and sew.

12. Sew the binding to the back of the quilt and add a label.

> Hint: In order to bind around the curved edges of this quilt, it is essential that the binding be cut on the bias instead of on the straight of grain. By cutting on the bias the fabric has a natural give that allows it to bend around the curves.

Making Continuous Bias Binding

1. Cut a square of fabric the size required for the length of binding. To calculate size of square for this quilt:

   2 1/2" x 395 = 962.5

   $\sqrt{962.5} = 31.02$

   You will need 32" x 32" square of fabric.

2. Pin the fabric on both sides and draw a diagonal line from corner to corner.

3. Cut on diagonal line and place the 2 pinned edges right sides together. The tails will overhang by ¼". Sew a ¼" seam.

4. Press the seam open.

5. Use the ruler to mark lines 2 ½" apart.

6. Make a tube by bringing the ends together with right sides facing. Offset the first line by one and match all the remaining lines.

7. Sew a ¼" seam. Press open seam.

8. Cut on the drawn line in a continuous manner creating one length of bias binding.

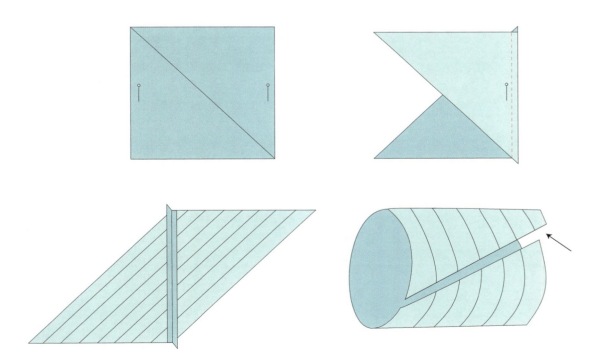

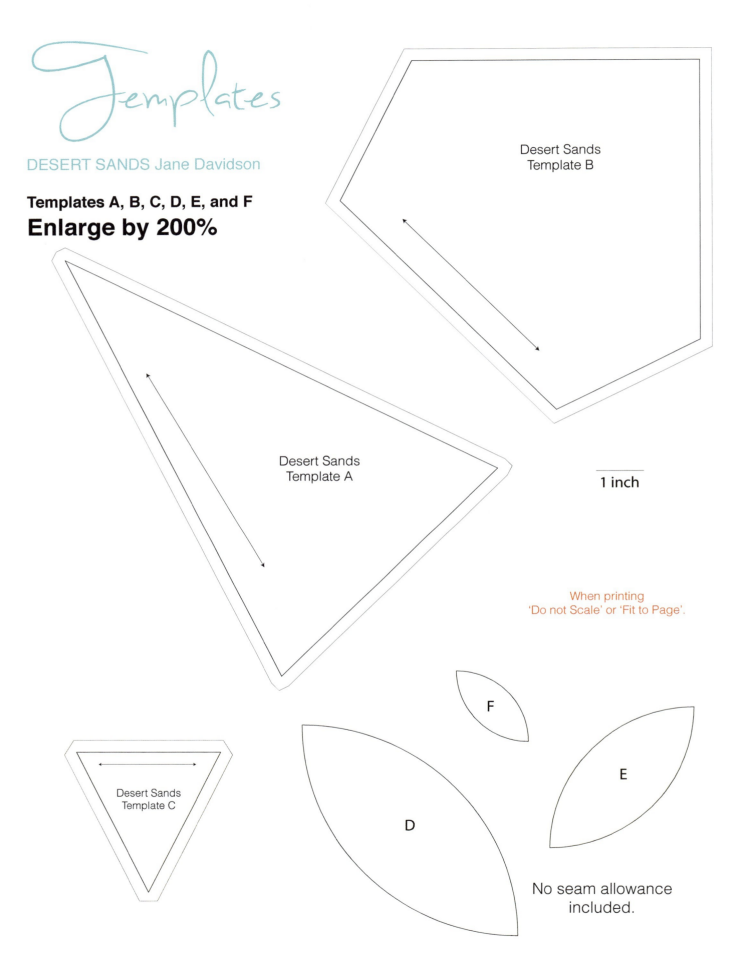

Templates

DESERT SANDS Jane Davidson

Templates A, B, C, D, E, and F
Enlarge by 200%

Desert Sands
Template B

Desert Sands
Template A

1 inch

When printing
'Do not Scale' or 'Fit to Page'.

Desert Sands
Template C

F

D

E

No seam allowance
included.

When printing
'Do not Scale' or 'Fit to Page'.

Templates A, B, C, D and Circle Templates
Enlarge by 200%

Circle Templates

No seam allowance
included.

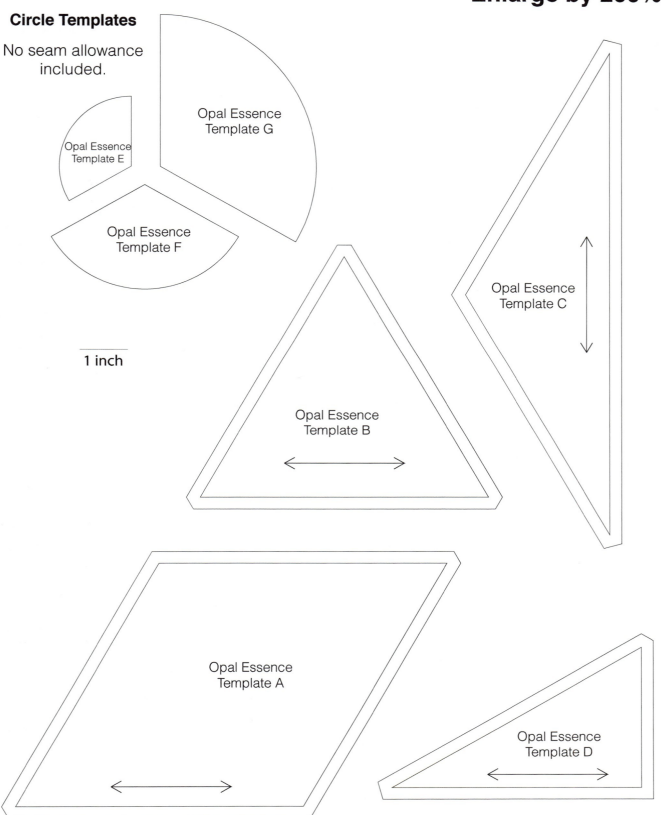

Opal Essence
Template G

Opal Essence
Template E

Opal Essence
Template F

Opal Essence
Template C

1 inch

Opal Essence
Template B

Opal Essence
Template A

Opal Essence
Template D

Templates A, B, and C
Enlarge by 200%

When printing
'Do not Scale' or 'Fit to Page'.

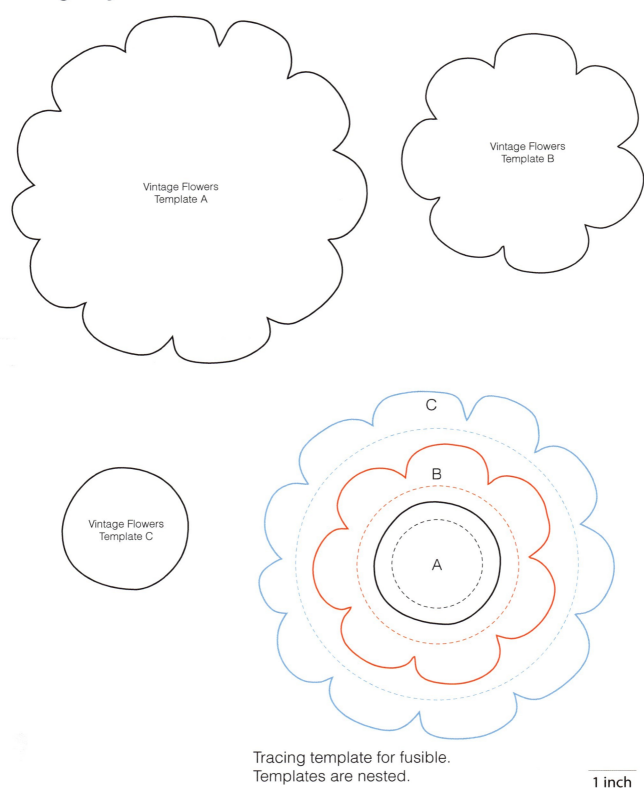

Vintage Flowers
Template A

Vintage Flowers
Template B

Vintage Flowers
Template C

C

B

A

Tracing template for fusible.
Templates are nested.

1 inch

ARROW TO THE HEART Charlotte Dumsney

Templates A and B
Enlarge by 400%

When printing
'Do not Scale' or 'Fit to Page'.

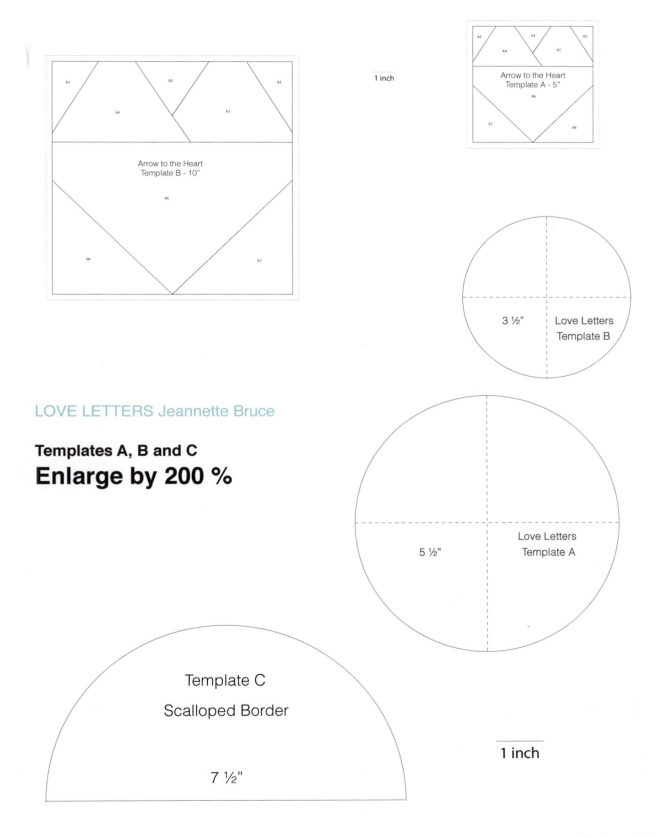

1 inch

A5 A3 A2
A4 A1

Arrow to the Heart
Template A - 5"

A6

A7 A8

Arrow to the Heart
Template B - 10"

A5 A3 A2
A4 A1

A6

A8 A7

3 ½"   Love Letters
Template B

LOVE LETTERS Jeannette Bruce

Templates A, B and C
Enlarge by 200 %

5 ½"   Love Letters
Template A

Template C

Scalloped Border

7 ½"

1 inch

When printing
'Do not Scale' or 'Fit to Page'.

Templates A, B, C, D, E and F
Enlarge by 200%

No seam allowance is required.

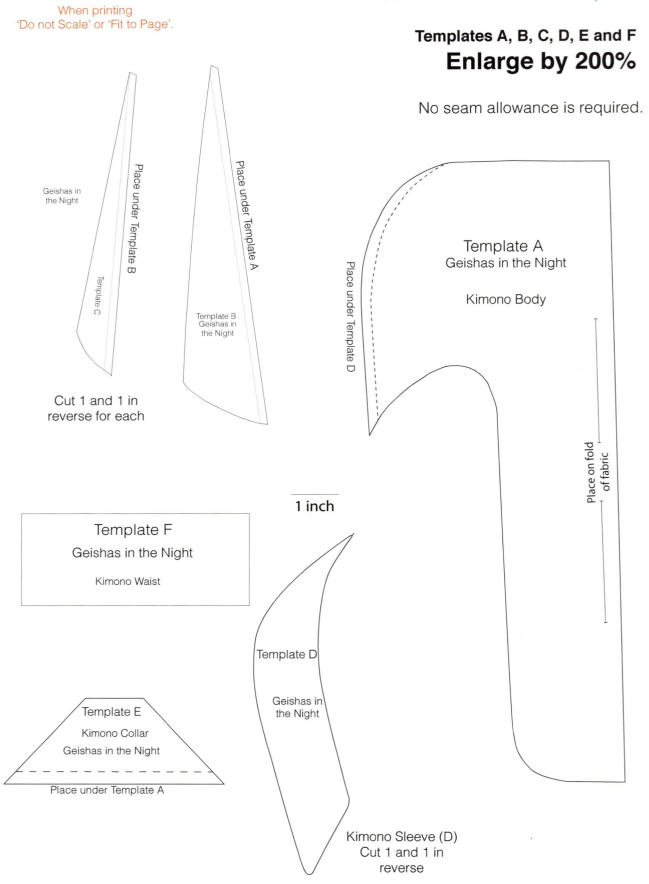

Geishas in
the Night

Place under Template B

Template C

Place under Template A

Template B
Geishas in
the Night

Cut 1 and 1 in
reverse for each

Template A
Geishas in the Night

Kimono Body

Place under Template D

Place on fold
of fabric

Template F

Geishas in the Night

Kimono Waist

1 inch

Template D

Geishas in
the Night

Template E

Kimono Collar
Geishas in the Night

Place under Template A

Kimono Sleeve (D)
Cut 1 and 1 in
reverse

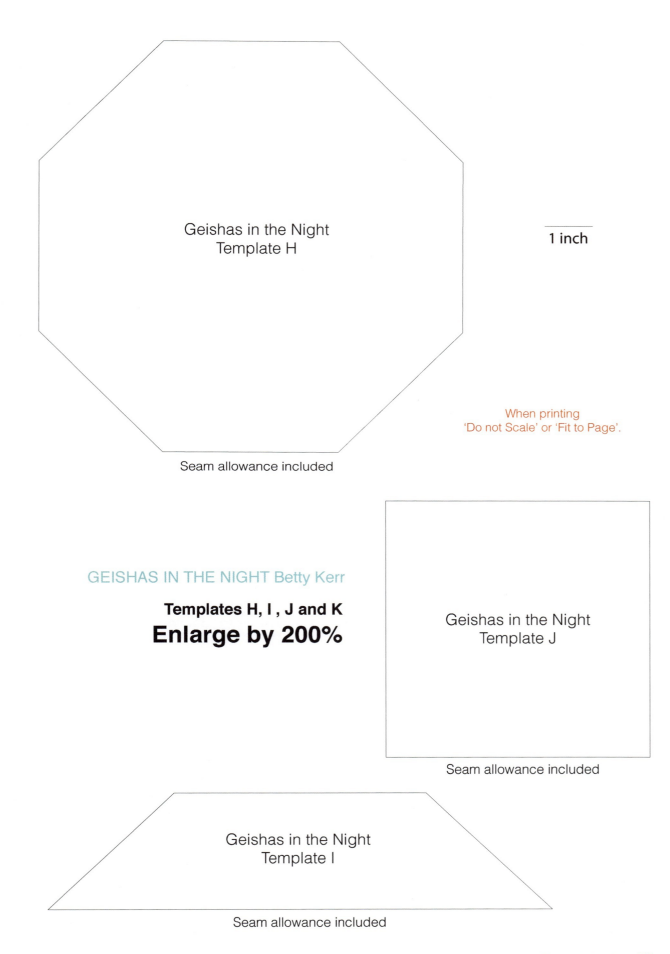

Geishas in the Night
Template H

1 inch

When printing
'Do not Scale' or 'Fit to Page'.

Seam allowance included

GEISHAS IN THE NIGHT Betty Kerr

Templates H, I , J and K
Enlarge by 200%

Geishas in the Night
Template J

Seam allowance included

Geishas in the Night
Template I

Seam allowance included

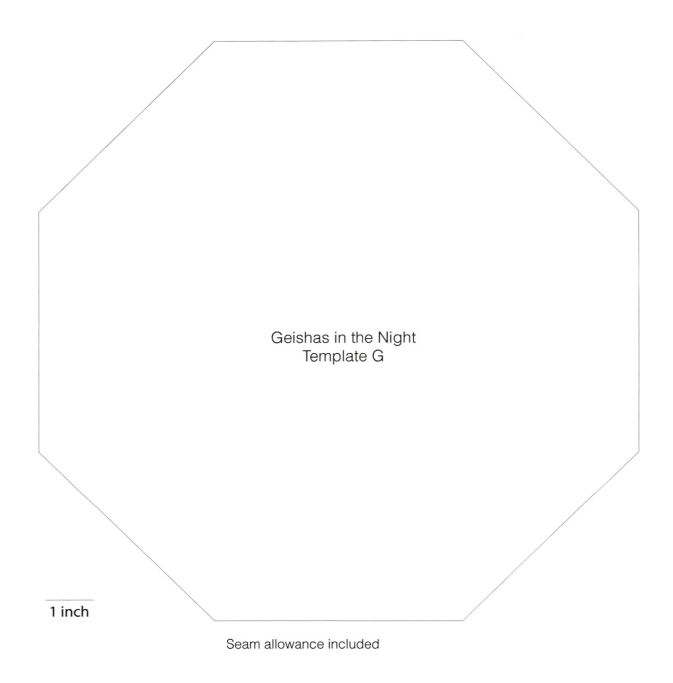

Geishas in the Night
Template G

1 inch

Seam allowance included

GEISHAS IN THE NIGHT Betty Kerr

Template G
Enlarge by 200%

Template K

Seam allowance has not been added

Sashiko Designs
Enlarge as indicated for each design

When printing
'Do not Scale' or 'Fit to Page'.

Noshi Ribbons - enlarge by 300%

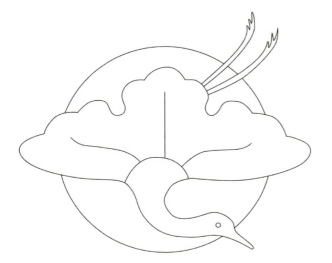

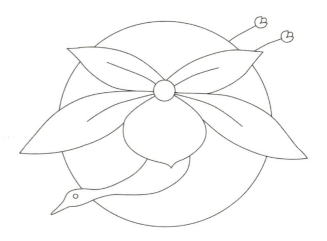

Cranes - Enlarge by 400%

Templates A and B
Enlarge by 200%

1 inch

Around the Rainbow
Template A - 3 ½"

Around the Rainbow
Template B - 5"

Foundation Templates A, B, C, D, E and F
Enlarge by 200%

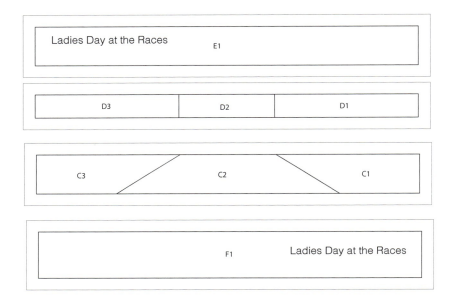

1 inch

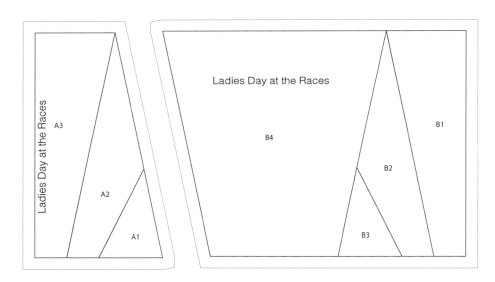

When printing
'Do not Scale' or 'Fit to Page'.

Templates B, C, D and E
Do Not Enlarge

When printing
'Do not Scale' or 'Fit to Page'.

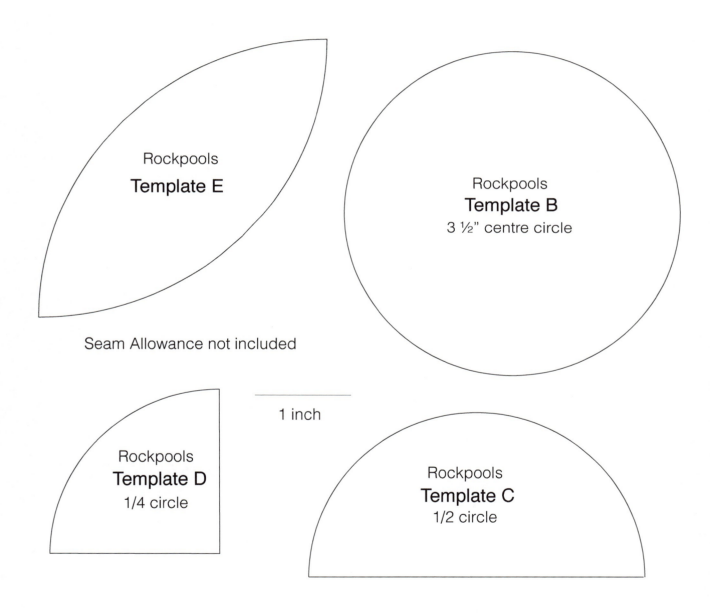

Rockpools
Template E

Rockpools
Template B
3 ½" centre circle

Seam Allowance not included

1 inch

Rockpools
Template D
1/4 circle

Rockpools
Template C
1/2 circle

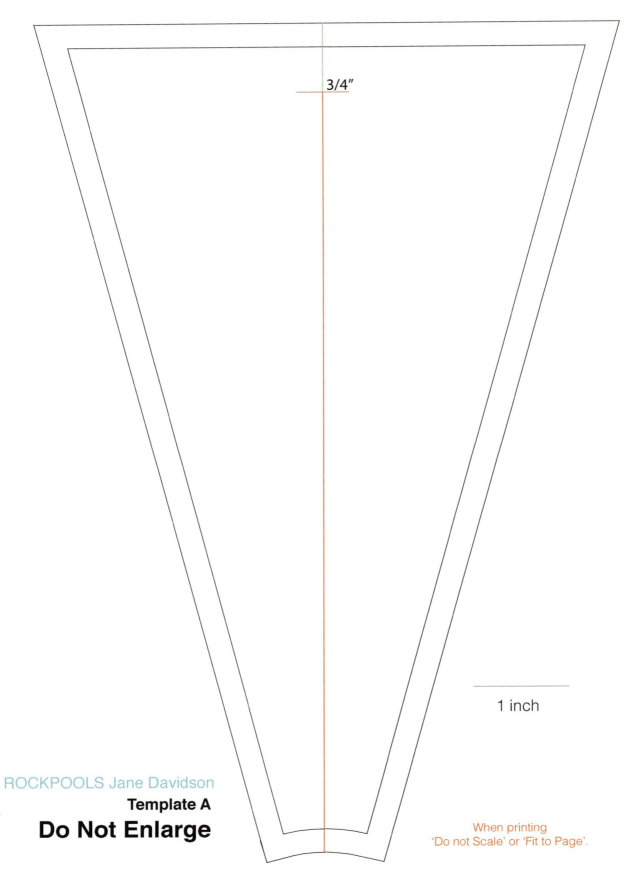

3/4"

1 inch

ROCKPOOLS Jane Davidson
Template A
Do Not Enlarge

When printing
'Do not Scale' or 'Fit to Page'.

ROCKPOOLS Jane Davidson

Template A - Paper Piecing Option
Enlarge by 200%

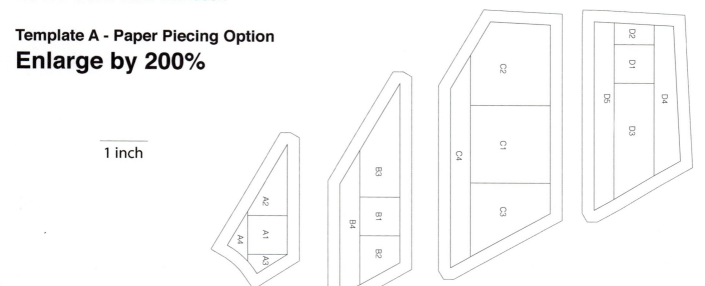

1 inch

RIC RAC RAZZAMATAZZ Rachaeldaisy

When printing
'Do not Scale' or 'Fit to Page'.

Templates A, B, and C
Enlarge by 200%

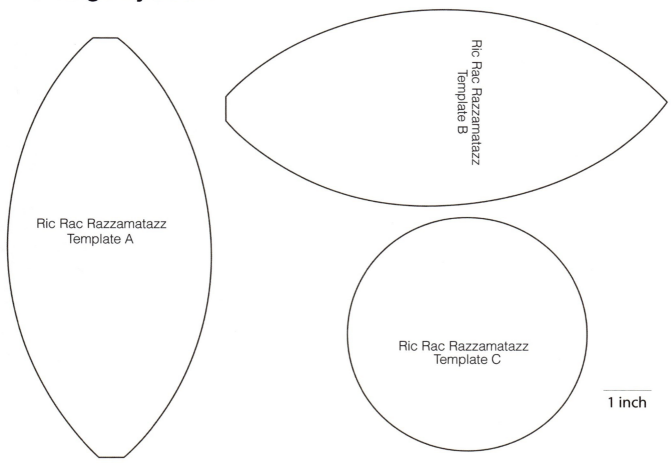

Ric Rac Razzamatazz
Template A

Ric Rac Razzamatazz
Template B

Ric Rac Razzamatazz
Template C

1 inch

Around the Rainbow

Danielle Aeuckens

Around the Rainbow

Danielle Aeuckens

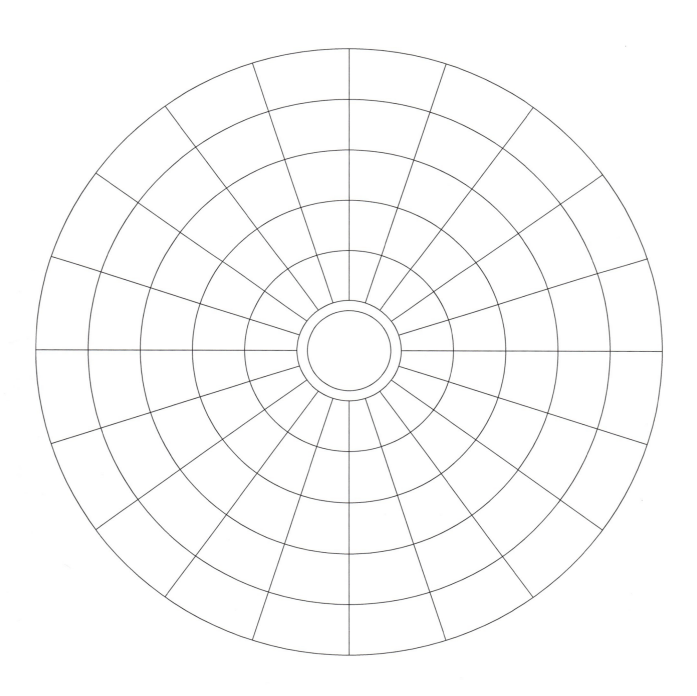

Opal Essence

Lorena Uriarte

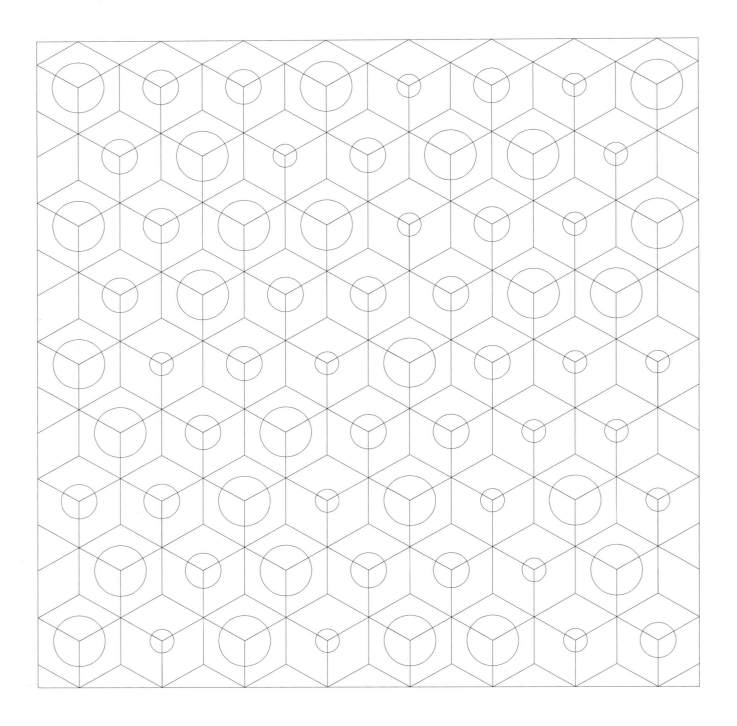

Ric Rac Razzamatazz

Rachaeldaisy

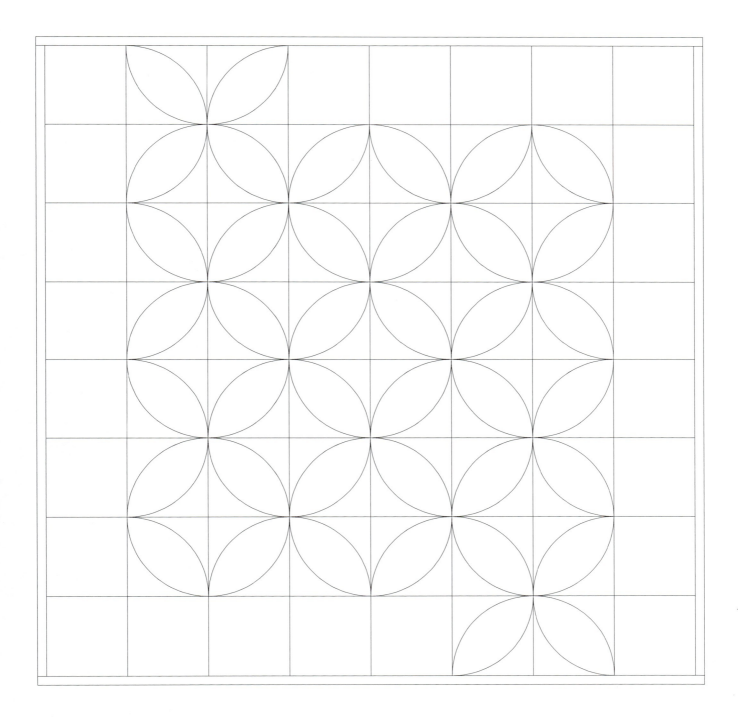

Designers

Danielle Aeuckens

Danielle has been crafting since she was old enough to hold a pair of knitting needles and grew up inspired by her grandmother, a master spinner, weaver, knitter and seamstress, and mother, a dressmaker and later a quilter. She made her first quilt around ten years ago but the obsession only took hold in the last four years. Her favourite techniques are hand appliqué, English paper piecing and machine and hand quilting. More recently, Danielle has began teaching others to quilt and knit and in 2013 opened an online fabric store Polka Dot Tea with her friend Jeannette Bruce. Danielle lives in Canberra with her husband and three children, who are very tolerant of the piles of fabric around the house and stray threads on the floor.

aeuckensd@gmail.com
mespetitselefants.blogspot.com

Lorena Uriarte

Lorena is an award winning quilt maker based in the Sydney beach side suburb of Maroubra. She teaches patchwork and quilting classes for children and adults. Lorena is always learning new techniques and trying new products that inspire her to design and make her own quilts.
Lorena has been quilting for 14 years and describes her style as strong on technique and colour. The vibrant, bright colours of her South American heritage and the clear light of her family home influence her fabric choices.
"It's rewarding to bring the pieces together accurately." Lorena says. "I find the challenge of making my quilt tops fit together like a giant jigsaw puzzle thrilling. The fact that it results in a wonderful warm quilt and a work of art is just the icing on the cake."
When not daydreaming about quilt making, Lorena is looking after her vegetable garden and teaching vegetarian cookery.

contact@lorenauriarte.com
www.lorenauriarte.com

Cathy Underhill

Cathy works under the alias Cabbage Quilts. Recently, Cathy left her job as a library officer to concentrate on her passion and obsession for quilting, design and textiles. Cathy adores creating projects with all the wonderful fabrics and threads available today. Cathy teaches at Treehouse Textiles, a lovely venture owned by the mother and daughter team, Emma and Sarah. Emma and Sarah have encouraged Cathy to pass on her passion for quilting and colour to others by a collaborative publication of a block of the month, Citrus Sweet Love.
Cathy has been published in many magazines and will be releasing her own patterns. Cathy lives on the Mornington peninsula in Victoria, and is often inspired by the beaches, wineries and countryside around her. She shares her life with her gorgeous husband and two awesome sons, and a funny Groodle (part poodle, part golden retriever) named Millie.

cabbagequilts@gmail.com
cabbagequilts.blogspot.com

Rachaeldaisy

Rachaeldaisy grew up in a family of visual artists and subsequently became a florist for 20 years. Thinking about colour and composition has always been a part of her life. When she was young she would spend school holidays with her grandmother who taught Rachaeldaisy to embroider, english paper piece and perform very basic dressmaking. When she reached her teenage years the sewing was more about altering thrifted clothes to suit Rachaeldaisy's idea of fashionable attire. A few years later she moved out of home and used her sewing machine for making curtains, cushions and the like. Fast forward to 2008 when some wonderful bright fabrics caught her eye and Rachaeldaisy knew she had to use them to make something. What could be easier than sewing squares together into a quilt... well, she pretty much did everything wrong when making that first quilt but by some magic it has held together and somewhere in those stitches she became hooked on quilting. Rachaeldaisy says, "The wonderful thing about quilting is there are always new fabrics to discover, new techniques to try, a world full of inspiration to keep things interesting and lots of friendly quilters to meet. "

rachaeldaisy@gmail.com
bluemountaindaisy.blogspot.com

Jeannette Bruce

Jeannette is an American transplant living on a sheep and cattle property on the Monaro Region of New South Wales with her husband and two young boys. After experimenting with the creative processes of making pottery, knitting and spinning wool, she found her mum's old sewing machine and decided to teach herself to quilt in 2005, just before moving to Australia. Making quilts kept her busy after moving to a rural community and since starting has made nearly 100 quilts. She now owns and operates a long arm quilting business and for the last two and half years in which she has quilted over 500 quilts for others during that time. She started long arm quilting with the desire to help people be able to finish their quilting projects as well as her own. Always the adventurer, Jeannette likes to experiment with all aspects of the quilting process and enjoys learning new techniques and in particular, experimenting with colour, which she finds a therapeutic process. Recently, she has started a online fabric shop, Polka Dot Tea, in partnership with Danielle Aeuckens, which continues to fuel her fabric obsession.

goneaussieheidi@gmail.com
goneaussiequilting.blogspot.com

Charlotte Dimsmen

Charlotte is the quilter behind Lawson and Lotti. She has been sewing since she was a little girl and used to play on her mothers sewing studio floor with scraps of fabric and vintage buttons. After school she studied fashion and textiles at university, which further cemented her love of designing. It was while travelling around Australia in 2004 that she learnt to quilt by her now mother-in-law. On her return to England, Charlotte taught Textile Technology in secondary school and continued sewing and quilting. In 2012 she won fashion designer of the year in British magazine Sew Hip's national competition. Her prize was a wonderful sewing machine, which she promptly packed up and brought back to Australia where she now lives. Charlotte now happily juggles her love of quilting with her other passions of clothing design, textile design and bringing up her three beautiful children. When she is not in her studio, she can be found walking with her husband and children on the wonderful Australian coastline, camping with the family or fuelling her addiction on Pinterest.

lawsonandlotti@live.com
lawsonandlotti.blogspot.com

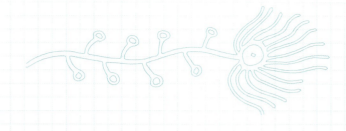

Betty Kerr

Betty's passion for sewing started at a very early age when she was taught to sew by her mother and sister. Betty loved sewing clothes for family and friends but after a friend introduced her to patchwork quilting, she was hooked! Betty had such fun playing with patterns and designs, scanning the wonderful books and learning the craft. Now, more than 20 years on, she still enjoys the sewing and especially taking on new patterns that will challenge her and encourage her to achieve the best design and work possible. In 2006 she moved to Singapore for 18 months. Not knowing a soul there Betty joined the Australian New Zealand club quilter's group to meet people and help in her transition to a new country. Betty's favourite quilt is her Singapore award winning colour wash of Steve Irwin holding a baby crocodile. It was made from over 5000 – 1" squares with over 75 colours.

betty@kerraustralia.com

Jane Davidson

Jane started quilting over 20 years ago by designing and hand piecing a queen sized quilt. Caught up in study and travel, it was not until 2010 did she rekindle her passion for quilting again. "I love everything about quilting and the quilting industry. I am so inspired by the enthusiasm and creativity I see everyday". A scientist at heart, Jane loves the engineering behind the quilt making process – the planning, the fabric selection, the designing and construction, and of course the quilting. She is always ready to challenge her skills when designing a new block or quilt. These days you can find Jane in her studio running a professional long-arm quilting service, teaching, designing and planning her next publication.

quiltjane@gmail.com
www.quiltjane.com

Acknowledgements

Self-publishing for the first time has been a wonderful experience. I would like to thank my family and friends for helping me on this journey. I would like to extend a special mention to all the designers for their hard work and the talented Kate Alexander for her excellent tuition and creative artistry. Thank you Mandy Ivastchenko, Tania Warren, Anne Maree Norris and Judith McLaughlin for all your patience, talent and support.

Starring the beautiful fabrics and notions from ....

Art Gallery Fabrics	www.artgalleryfabrics.com
Moda United Notions	www.unitednotions.com
Simplicity	www.simplicity.com
Free Spirit Fabrics	www.freespiritfabric.com
Robert Kaufman Fabrics/RK Studio	www.robertkaufman.com
Michael Miller Fabrics	www.michaelmillerfabrics.com

Quilt flat shot photography by Mark Heriot Photography

41468213R00052